To Janet—
Best always—
Betty

D1400373

THE BUSY PERSON'S GUIDE TO BALANCE AND BOUNDARIES

Betty Hill Crowson

authorHOUSE®

AuthorHouse™
1663 Liberty Drive
Bloomington, IN 47403
www.authorhouse.com
Phone: 1-800-839-8640

Published by AuthorHouse 12/17/2013

ISBN: 978-1-4918-4044-3 (sc)
ISBN: 978-1-4918-4043-6 (hc)
ISBN: 978-1-4918-4042-9 (e)

Library of Congress Control Number: 2013921692

Acknowledgements...

Writing a book can be a very lonely process, always more difficult and taking much longer than one can ever imagine. This was my second go at such an undertaking and, although not quite as daunting as the first time, *The Busy Person's Guide to Balance and Boundaries* would never have seen the light of day were it not for the support that I have received from so many wonderful people.

First of all, I would like to acknowledge and thank Ken and Donna Wright for their kind generosity in allowing me to spend the fall and winter months living and writing in the most perfect little cottage by the sea. I would also like to thank my closest group of women friends who continue to inspire me by the ways in which they lead their own lives—you know who you are. I especially want to mention Jane Militello, whose words of encouragement and faith in my work have carried me through some very tedious and self-doubting days. And, of course, I never could have written this book without the wisdom gained from working with my clients, as well as the many wonderful women and men who fill up my retreats and workshops. Without a doubt, you are all my greatest motivation for continuing to suit up and show up for the work I love. And I thank you for that.

I also want to acknowledge those who have had first-hand involvement in shaping this book: Ann Ledva and Lisa Argenio-Brenner who have both been champions of support, while always ready and willing to take a look and offer a suggestion or two; Kim O'Rourke for her great eye at catching mistakes; my sister Judith Parks for double-checking; Lee Toth for the spot-on graphics; Bill Wood, Ashala Gabriel, Joan Dim, and Rosemary Williams for taking the time to read and endorse my work; Barbara Graham for giving it a final check-over; and a huge thanks to my twenty-four year old son, Rob, and Emma Holt Sawyer, for putting together a great cover design!

But most of all, I want to express my sincere appreciation for my dear friend, Marilynn Pysher, who has now encouraged and supported me through the writing of two books! I never could have done it without you, Marilynn—which is why I dedicate this book to you.

Contents

Introduction

I was born into busy-ness and raised in chaos. At the time of my birth, my parents had just purchased a dairy farm in Maine which required all of their time and attention. I already had an older sister and, with other siblings quickly added to the mix, I became sandwiched in-between kids, cows, chickens, and chores. And while you could never accuse either one of my parents of being abusive or even unloving, they were definitely very, very busy.

In the beginning, early childhood photos depict me happy, a child of light; a smiling towhead usually hand in hand with Bobby, my younger brother, with whom I shared the same age during one week every March. We were bonded in a very special way, inseparable right from the start. With two hard working but rather inaccessible parents, I think we imprinted upon one another. There is nothing that could have prepared any of us for his tragic drowning at the age of seven. On that hot August afternoon, life as I knew it forever changed. It was as if a dark heavy cloak descended upon me and I became overwhelmed with grief, confusion, and anxiety. What made it even worse was the fact that there were no immediate resources to help me understand and to cope with this horrific tragedy. In fact, in their own attempts at dealing with this devastating loss, those around me became even busier and less emotionally available.

From that moment on, I didn't feel safe. Consumed with a host of inner feelings and emotions which I have come to define as "cosmic unrest," I felt insecure, disconnected, fearful, lost, and lonely. At the same time, I experienced a chronic yearning for something I couldn't name, and a huge need for relief from all of the above.

At first, I found solace and refuge in reading and fantasy. Hours were spent pretending to be Superwoman or the Lone Ranger, or fantasizing about far-off lands and magical, romantic adventures. As I became an adolescent, my biggest concerns were to stop feeling so awkward in my own skin, to be happy, and to have somebody—*anybody*—love me. And although I appeared to function well enough during these middle and high school years, I didn't feel okay at all. I lived with a chronic sense of impending doom as well as a feeling that I had somehow missed out on the "directions" for living.

Upon graduation, my grades and SAT scores were high enough to get into several colleges, but my self-esteem was not. So when my friends went off to higher learning, I settled for less, becoming a waitress and eventually a bartender. My emotional confusion and distorted self-perception were already calling the shots, and continued to do so for several more years.

Working in restaurants and bars throughout my twenties gave me ample opportunity to get relief from my "cosmic unrest" in another way—by the use and, as it so happened, *overuse* of alcohol. Drinking actually worked in the beginning. It eased my deep-rooted anxiety and gave me hope that I could live in this world with some degree of comfort. But there is a funny thing about depending upon any substance for relief: It will eventually turn on you.

During these same years, I also attempted to placate my restless longing and inner void by pursuing creative enterprises. I painted, wrote poetry, threw pots on a wheel. Whatever I was involved in, I was completely obsessive about—until I wasn't. And then it was put aside. All or nothing, I would go from one extreme to the other. I knew little about balance.

I dealt with relationships in much the same fashion. Looking for the attention, affection, and approval that I had never received as a child, I was convinced that getting these needs met would somehow "fix" me. Driven by this misconception, I went from man to man, relationship to relationship, never staying too long, incapable of setting or maintaining boundaries, and not having a clue how to work through issues when they presented themselves. As they always did.

My favorite cry throughout this time was, "Where's the party?" Convinced as I was that the right man or the right environment or the right *something* was the magical answer to all of my problems, I became a blur of misguided motion. Yet, wherever I was, I was usually thinking I should be somewhere else. Whoever I was with, I thought I should be with somebody else. And so I continued to go nowhere just as fast as I could get there.

Luckily for me, not everything went wrong. One of my male choices turned out to be exactly what I needed. Robert was kind, loving, and consistent. I felt safe with him. We dated long distance for several years before eventually marrying. It was shortly thereafter, through a series of "coincidences," that I woke up to the fact that alcohol was doing far more to me than <u>for</u> me. It was at this time that I was to take my last drink.

This coincided with my being introduced to the idea of spirituality as a way of life; of looking within for answers as well as seeking help from some Higher Source or Power. And despite the fact that, for reasons unknown to me even today, I had a terrible prejudice towards anything of this nature, I immediately began to follow a different path. As I did, my entire consciousness underwent a psychic shift. This did not come one minute too soon, for a few short months later, the unthinkable happened: Robert was diagnosed with terminal brain cancer. My husband, whom I adored above all else, died a few weeks after our first wedding anniversary. The heavy black cloak of despair fell round me once more. Even now after all these years, there are no words to convey my sense of loss and grief at this time. Talk about needing relief!

It is nothing short of miraculous that, when this happened, I really understood that alcohol and drugs were not an option; that the use of either would only serve to exacerbate rather than alleviate my pain. I also knew that to quickly try and "replace" my husband with another man was not going to be an answer either. My grief was too intense for that. But when you don't know what to do, you generally do what you know. And the message I had received so many years ago was that when tragedy strikes, you get busy. This is what I did. Supported by a society that doesn't know any better, I got *super busy.*

Within a few months, I became a full-time college student with a twelve hour a week practicum to boot. I gave up smoking and started running. Over the next four years, I studied, dated, attended numerous body/soul retreats and conferences, ran races, and graduated Summa Cum Laude. I looked great and so did my life. Yet, I would wake up in the mornings with that heavy cloak surrounding my heart. Driving down the road on a beautiful sunny day, I would be consumed with a sense of this little girl inside of me, sobbing. I didn't know what was happening or why. Here I was, doing everything "right," yet feeling anything but.

Gratefully, at this time, I got into therapy where it was revealed that I was in tremendous grief; the unhealed grief of losing my husband, the pain of losing my brother so many years before, as well as several other losses which had been unacknowledged and unhealed along the way. Thus I began the process of healing my deep inner sorrow. Yet, begin is all I did. It just seemed too self-centered to focus on all this "stuff." Besides, I had things to do, people to help, places to go.

Once again, I got *real busy*. I met and married an Episcopalian priest, worked as a social worker, and became convinced that being all things to those around me was the role I was meant to play. Eventually, we had a baby boy whom we named Robert. From the outside, my life looked good; really good. And although the joy of motherhood cannot be minimized, I was still going as fast as I could go in an attempt to outrun my inner life; the fear and the grief that were constantly nipping at my heels.

As it so happened, my son's birth was the beginning of physical and emotional challenges that seemed to come in a never-ending series. To begin with, due to a long-standing precancerous condition, it was necessary for me to undergo a hysterectomy when my son was a year old. While I was recovering from this, my husband developed a heart problem which resulted in several complications. During his recovery, a huge schism occurred in the parish where he was a priest. Stress was piled upon stress.

In the midst of coping with and trying to take care of everything, I began to intuitively sense that something wasn't quite right with me physically. It was nothing I could put my finger on, but I just felt like I was sick somehow. It wasn't long before a routine mammogram revealed that my intuition was correct. My son wasn't even three years old when I was diagnosed with breast cancer. It just didn't seem fair.

This new reality stopped me in my tracks. It got my attention at a depth that nothing previously had been able to touch. And as I began physical recovery, I also found it necessary to enter into a deeper and far more significant emotional and spiritual recovery as well. Finally, I put my chronic busy-ness and need-to-please aside, replacing them with self-care and intentionality. The Universe assisted big-time by putting the right people directly on my path. One of these was a wonderful and insightful Jungian therapist with whom I spent the next three years. If I were to sum up the work Dr. Eckles and I did, it was this: I learned how to get over myself in order to find my *Self*. With his guidance and support, I was able to get through and beyond my fear, grief, and sense of separateness in order to access those many "rooms" within which he assured me were there: wisdom, insight, intuition, and knowledge of myself as both insignificant and magnificent. This discovery process was neither short nor easy. Yet, it was work that ultimately allowed me to find everything I had always been seeking, and far, far *more*.

I share my story because I know that many of you will identify with it; perhaps not with the actual events, but certainly with the inner feelings and confusion. And perhaps more importantly, I believe you might identify with the frustration of distracting yourself with behaviors, habits, and busy-ness that may momentarily appease or cover up issues, but do nothing to actually address them.

It has been many years now since I spent this time with Dr. Eckles; years in which life has presented situations that have been predictable, as well as difficult. I have lost both of my parents, my son has grown and no longer needs me in the same ways, I divorced after 23 years of marriage (two nice people with irreconcilable differences), and I continually face the challenges of growing older and staying balanced in a society that often places little value on either.

Life has also unfolded in some surprising and wonderful ways. My work under the trademark of *The Joy is in the Journey*® has grown and evolved. I have become known and appreciated, especially throughout the Northeast, as a holistic life coach, motivational speaker, spiritual retreat director, and author. My previous book, *The Joy is in the Journey: A Woman's Guide through Crisis and Change*, has been able to guide thousands of women through difficult transitional times, and I have been blessed to meet and work with many wonderful groups and individuals. Throughout it all, my primary purpose has remained one and the same: to help men and women get unstuck and move forward; to get over and beyond those many things that drive and drain them, in order to find their Real Selves and true purpose. It is this intention that motivated the writing of *The Busy Person's Guides*.

The truth is, we all have these "rooms" within us of which Dr. Eckles spoke. Yet, we have become so incredibly busy that we feel little or no connection to the life that we are living, let alone to ourselves. We are so distracted and caught up in "doing" that we have lost sight of what really matters. It is way past time to change this dynamic.

Ask yourself these questions:

- Are you constantly running on empty?
- Is it second-nature for you to feel overwhelmed, over-extended, and/or under-appreciated?
- When asked to do something, do you say "yes," even when you know it will put you over the edge?
- Have you relegated yourself to low man on the totem pole?
- Do you consider it your job to fix or try and make others happy?
- Are your negative thoughts and emotions draining your enthusiasm and energy?
- Do you have a habit of finding fault with yourself?
- Do you often think "something is wrong with this picture" but feel powerless over changing the situation?
- Do you keep telling yourself that this year/summer/holiday will be different, but it never is?
- Have you lost sight of who you really are and what is your ultimate purpose?

If you answered yes to any of these, *The Busy Person's Guides* were written for you! This first book, *The Busy Person's Guide to Balance and Boundaries,* will start you off in the right direction. By leading you through a process for getting your feet back under you, it sets the playing field for recovering some very necessary time and energy. It gives you the tools for catching your breath and freeing up some space in order to do a little soul searching. At the same time, it provides the basis and foundation necessary to undergo the work of the second in this series, *The Busy Person's Guide to Inner Healing.* It is here where you will learn how to identify, address, and resolve those underlying issues which have driven you to be so out of balance in the first place! The third book, *The Busy Person's Guide to Joy and Fulfillment,* will take you one step further into where you want to be. Not frantic, frazzled, and frustrated, but confident, relaxed, fulfilled, and connected at a very deep level, not only with yourself, but with significant others as well.

It all begins here and now. And although this process as a whole may sound like a *huge stretch* from today's reality, it is not. There is a reason it has been divided into three separate books. The work it presents is both manageable as well as doable. And it has proven successful in my own life as well as in the lives of countless men and women whom I have counseled over the years. It will work for you if you work it. It really is that simple.

So take a breath. Sit back. Relax. I will be with you every step of this journey. If you can have the willingness to embrace the process as presented, you will be amazed at the results. This simple outlined path will empower you to find, utilize, and celebrate those many places inside of you which have been patiently awaiting your discovery.

Part One:
Create Personal Balance

Ask anybody how they are these days and the answer is almost always the same: "I'm so busy!"

Yes, we are busy, distracted, overextended, out of balance, and getting more so every day. We race from home to work, from event to event, from one obligation to the next. We keep piling stuff onto our plates without ever taking anything off. And we allow others to do the same, to our plate! We have become so accustomed to feeling overwhelmed, under-appreciated, off-kilter, and exhausted, we think it is normal.

Some of us are even addicted to our overly-committed lifestyles. We cite the fact that it's good to be busy. Or we make excuses for being frantic and frenzied. After all, if you had my life, husband, finances, job, and so forth, you'd be out of balance too! And, besides, we think there is nothing we can do to change things, at least not now. Maybe later—after this last push at work, or our children graduate, or when we become financially secure, or turn a certain age, or retire. So we just keep on keeping on, only to briefly surface every now and then, wondering how summer went by so fast, how the kids grew up so soon, how we got so old, or how we managed to get through another season, holiday, or year without even noticing.

Far too often, we find that our head is in one place and our feet in another. Pulled in many directions at the same time, we end up confusing motion for action, even though the difference between the two is enormous. *Action is deliberate, intentional, and well thought-out. Motion, on the other hand, is similar to being a wind-up toy in the corner.*

And it is often fueled by an underlying driven-ness. That's right—we are driven: driven by our attempts to make things look good at any cost; driven by our need to keep up with the Joneses; driven by our financial insecurity; driven by our desire to please everybody; driven by an urgency to outrun our inner feelings of pain, grief, guilt, and shame; driven from an inner conviction that we somehow don't quite measure up.

In many cases, we have become our own worst enemy. We tend to force solutions, often before their time; our self-will can run riot; and we over-do in too many areas to mention. And even when we convince ourselves that we're doing just fine, the minute some slow driver pulls out in front of us, or the kids spill chocolate milk all over the carpet, or we are presented with an unexpected issue at work, our over-reactions can be so intense and inappropriate that they shock even us.

Of course, every now and then we surface long enough to get a glimpse of the absolute insanity of our out-of-balance lifestyles. But what do we do with these moments of clarity? Do we pay attention, make a concerted effort to slow down, step back, regroup, and take a deep breath? Not usually. Most times we just push through and do the next thing on the list; the same list that never quite gets completed; the list that makes it impossible for us to enjoy guilt-free downtime.

Probably the biggest consequence of being overly-busy and out of balance is that we are not who we would wish to be. We don't always act like we want to, feel like we want to, or relate to others in the ways we would prefer. Often, we feel alone and separate; far removed from the knowledge of ourselves as part of something larger and greater, and light years away from our personal truth.

Clearly, it is time to get our feet back under us; to restore or create some balance. And although this is only the tip of the iceberg, it is absolutely essential that we begin here. There will be other issues to address as we go along, but we can't get to them until we first get our mental, physical, and emotional busy-ness under better control and in greater balance.

The good news is, we finally have directions on how to do this. So let's get started. And, seriously, if not now, when?

When we are overly-busy,
we often confuse
action with motion.

Chapter One: What are you *Doing?*

Before we begin, let's understand a few things:

- Many of us have become so busy that we often feel little or no connection to our own lives.
- To think that someday in the future we will "get our act together" is magical thinking. *Now* is the time to do this, not later, after, when, if...
- Nobody benefits by our being overextended, overwhelmed, exhausted, and/or emotionally off-kilter—nobody. (If we think this doesn't apply to us, we might ask somebody who lives or works with us!)
- There are steps we can and must take in order to recover or create greater personal balance.

Obviously, we can't do much until we have a clear picture of what needs to change. So a good place to begin this process is by looking at what we are so busy doing. In other words, what currently consumes our time, energy, hours, days, weeks, and even months? What is on all of these plates we are spinning in the air?

We need to take an inventory; an assessment that looks at two things—what uses and drains our time and energy, and what refills and re-energizes us. This process is similar to determining one's financial condition. We all know that if we put more money into a bank account than we take out, we enjoy the freedom of having a surplus. This feels good. We are ready for an emergency. Our stress is greatly reduced from not only having enough, but having something to spare, a little extra—just in case.

On the other hand, when we withdraw more than we put in, our funds become exhausted. Our checkbook is out of balance, our checks may bounce, and in some cases, we become hopelessly broke.

This same banking principle can be easily applied to our physical expenditure of energy. Energy which consistently goes out without being replaced or replenished eventually runs out of steam. When we keep doing and giving, without benefit of refilling, we end up giving from the core, rather than any surplus. When this happens, our lives and our bodies become stressed and begin to break down on a daily basis. Rather than human beings, we become human "doings," and we suffer for it. We can have difficulty sleeping, live with excessive anxiety, and experience all types of physical disorders.

We really must change this dynamic. And we can—one baby step at a time. The following exercise (borrowed from this author's previous book, *The Joy is in the Journey: A Woman's Guide through Crisis and Change*), is a great place to begin. And although it may take a few minutes to complete, it will be time well spent. So even if you think you already know the answers, do the following the way it is laid out. As you do, more will absolutely be revealed.

Exercise 1: Make a List

This first exercise helps us look at what currently consumes our time and energy. Take your own personal inventory by writing down on the left side of the chart below (Outgoing Energy), what you typically do in a day; just a list of chores, obligations, and commitments. Don't worry about the right side of the chart right now; we will address that in another section.

Time/Energy Awareness Chart

outgoing energy (-)	incoming energy (+)

As you make this list, be sure to include routine activities such as working, commuting, shopping, child or animal care, checking emails, car pooling, and/or family commitments. Also make note of things like reading, watching television, talking with friends, exercising, playing games on the computer, and so forth.

After compiling your initial list, pick one day to become an observer in your own life; a day dedicated to really paying attention to and keeping track of how much time you actually spend doing various things. Keep a notebook with you and write down the specifics. For instance:

- Working outside of the home—8 hours
- Commuting—1 hour
- Doing household chores—2 hours
- Watching television—3 hours
- Talking with friends on the telephone—1 hour
- Spending time on the computer/Internet—2 hours

At the end of the day, check this new list against the original list. Any surprises?

After doing this exercise, notice if any of the things on your list are new additions to your time/energy usage. For example, did you recently take on extra hours at work, enroll in a college course or two, bring home a new baby or pet, begin caring for an elderly or sick friend or relative, start a different job with a longer commute? Are you newly divorced or widowed with increased responsibilities? Have you received a recent diagnosis that requires additional appointments or tests? Or has something recently been removed from your life? Highlight any recent changes.

When you finish writing, try to step outside of yourself and do a quick assessment of your "outgoing energy." Be as objective as you can. We are only gathering information and there is no need to make any kind of negative judgment, which would only be a further waste of energy! You are encouraged to be "curious not critical," a phrase that will be repeated often throughout this book.

Now, looking at your list, honestly ask yourself the following:

- Am I doing too much in general?
- Am I doing *way* too much?
- Are my expectations of what I should be able to accomplish in a day realistic or far from it? (Now, be honest!)
- Do I typically take care of everyone else's needs before my own? Am I paying a price for this, physically or emotionally?
- On a normal day, can I identify feeling any of the following: overwhelmed, resentful, exhausted, angry, anxious, over-extended, and/or under-appreciated?
- If I recently took on new chores or responsibilities, whether in the home, office, or community, have I given anything up in order to accommodate these?
- If circumstances are such that I have been left with a huge void in a once-full life, am I going as fast as I can, trying to fill it just for the sake of filling it?

When we are over-extended, everything becomes a chore, even the pleasurable. We've all been there.

"Do I *have to* go to my book club?"

"I wish I hadn't told the guys I'd play poker tonight."

"I can't believe I said I would go to the play!"

When we are over-extended,
everything becomes a chore;
even the pleasurable.

Or perhaps we are one of those who is currently living with the opposite problem—too little to do because of a major loss. When this is the case, the tendency here can be to try to fill the empty spaces with just about *anything* in order to escape the accompanying feelings. While that is not necessarily a bad thing to do, especially in the beginning, it is not meant to become a way of life. This book's sequel on inner healing will address many of these issues. In the meantime, working on balance and boundaries is still the next right thing to do.

Exercise 2: Take One Thing Off of Your Plate

This next exercise, while extremely simple, will not be easy for most. It requires us to make a decision to stop doing SOMETHING; to remove at least one thing from our never-ending list of "what we typically do in any given day."

Some of us won't even know where to begin. Perhaps we've convinced ourselves that there is nothing we can change; no task we can eliminate or delegate. If this is your case, you may need to delve a little deeper. So take another look at your "outgoing energy" list in relationship to the following questions, and be willing to get really honest. Remember, you do have choices!

- Are there things on this list that really don't need to be done now? Could they possibly be put off for another time, another week, month, or even another year? This is not to be confused with procrastination but refers to becoming "right-sized" with your self-expectations.

- Is there anything on this list that somebody else in the family/office/neighborhood/church could or should be doing? Can you ask them? Is the thought of doing that difficult? Has this been a lifelong issue?
- Do you believe that just because you can do something well, that you're the one who is supposed to do it?
- Do you believe that just because somebody asks you to do something, you need to say yes? Could this be related to ego, people-pleasing, or the need to be in control of things? (Not to worry: We will deal with all of these in following chapters.)
- Is part of the reason you don't delegate because you're afraid other people won't do it the "right" way or at the right time? What would be the worst thing that could happen?
- Do you tend to feel anxious if every moment of your life isn't filled with activity? Or do you feel guilty if you're not busy doing *something*? Do you know where these feelings come from?
- Do you have unrealistic expectations of what you *should* be able to accomplish in a day? Do you often end up disappointed in yourself when you don't accomplish everything?
- When *was* the last time you enjoyed guilt-free downtime?

Once again, as you answer these questions, there is no need to be self-critical. Be curious instead. In fact, as you move through this book, you will undoubtedly find that much of your tendency to be overly-busy is related to boundary issues which we will be addressing further on.

However, in the meantime, consider taking at least ONE thing off your daily "to do" list. Are you willing to do this? To either let a specific task or obligation or commitment go completely, or to delegate it to somebody else—without becoming overly-concerned with whether or not they are doing it "your way?"

If you're struggling with this, the following exercise should provide some greater clarity.

Exercise 3: Ask Yourself What Really Matters

Those first two exercises were intended to just get us moving in a different direction—towards balance. However, the extent to which we take the suggestions put forth will undoubtedly come down to how motivated we really are to change, or how awakened we become to our *need* to change. So, let's take a moment now to ask ourselves what are probably the most important questions we can ever ask: "What are my basic values and authentic priorities? In the larger scheme of things, what really matters to me?"

What are your priorities? What do you truly care about? Health, family, spirituality, career, creativity, travel, intellectual stimulation, church, networking, increasing your visibility in the larger world, being of service, having a partner, writing, completing a specific goal? What really matters?

Simply put, if you knew that your life was time-limited (which of course it is), what do you want to be doing with your time and energy? Take a few moments to list at least five things that you deem important. Write them down. Once again, think deeply and be honest with yourself.

Now comes the *really* important part. After completing this list of personal priorities, compare it to your list of what you are currently doing. Do the two resemble each other at all? Or is the daily "to do" list far removed from what really matters to you? If so, it should be very evident that *something* needs to change! And it doesn't have to be a huge change; just a small course correction will begin to shift the energy. Don't worry; more is going to be revealed as you go along. For right now, you're doing great!

Be Curious—
Not Critical.

Chapter Two: Regroup, Refill, Recover

Now we need to find ways in which to increase our "incoming energy." We may have already determined that some of the same things that require our time and energy also energize us in return, such as exercise or time spent with friends or family. Writing our list may have also highlighted some task or commitment of time that we are willing to let go of, or delegate. We also took action by asking ourselves and writing down "what really matters." Comparing these priorities to our daily to-do list further increased our awareness.

It is now time to go one step further by learning, and eventually utilizing, practices that will help renew and re-energize us. This is how we begin filling in the right side of our Time Energy Awareness chart. This will prove a great deal more challenging than the left side did, primarily because it involves something with which many of us are not all that familiar—self-care. In fact, we may not even know what self-care implies. So let's keep this really simple by considering that self-care refers to *developing and maintaining actions, attitudes, and habits which, rather than add or create stress, promote balance and well-being instead.* Self-care boosts energy levels, elevates moods, clears up confusion, and increases self-esteem. It involves giving ourselves the same time, kindness, respect, and nurturing that we so often give others.

Self-care is not about whipping ourselves into shape. After all, we've tried that with little or no long-term success. So why not take another approach? Instead of beating ourselves into conformity, how about nurturing ourselves into well-being?

The best time to begin self-care is always first thing in the morning. Before racing helter-skelter into action, or should we say "motion," we must make/take intentional time to pause, reflect, and think about what we are planning to do and why. Simply put, *the way in which we begin our day will determine how well, or not, we will live it.* Taking time to think prior to "doing" is the beginning of increased consciousness. It is one of the most powerful changes we can ever make.

This morning practice will not demand a huge block of time. We only need five, maybe ten minutes, to pause, consider the day ahead, mentally envision our obligations and commitments, and perhaps even review some of these previous questions:

- Are there things I'm planning to squeeze in today that really don't need to be done now? Could they possibly be put off for another time, another week, month, or year?
- Is there anything on this list I could ask somebody else to do? Can I delegate it?
- Do I have unrealistic expectations on how much I "should" be able to accomplish today? Can I make a decision just for today, not to "should" all over myself?

If we can develop some discipline around this practice of becoming conscious—in other words, considering what we're planning to do and why *before* jumping into our day—we increase our chances tenfold for taking action rather than just getting caught up running in circles. At the same time, we increase our probability for acting like human beings rather than human doings. And we will begin to expend our time and energy on things that really matter, instead of simply taking care of business. This is the very beginning of healthy self-care, and when our own side of the street is in balance, the whole world benefits.

There are several other behaviors and actions which fall under the umbrella of healthy self-care. The following pages will look at some of these. Take time with the suggestions. Don't just read through them quickly, but really evaluate which ones you may currently be using, and which ones could use some additional attention.

Remember to breathe

It's amazing how many of us have actually forgotten how to breathe properly! Without being aware of it, our first reaction to any kind of stress, discord, or anxiety is almost universally the same: our shoulders start to hunch up, our hands begin to clench, and our breathing becomes shallow, at times to such an extent that we hyperventilate or even have an anxiety attack!

So easy does it. Take a deep breath right now. Breathe. Relax. Slow down. There is no rush. Don't make this book just another thing "to do." In fact, let's take a moment to practice the centering breath. It only takes two minutes and is a wonderful de-stressing tool which can be done

Self-care is not about
whipping ourselves into shape.
It involves nurturing
ourselves into well-being.

anywhere, anytime. It not only stops the cycle of stress, but it also reduces anxiety, and curbs anger. It is certainly worth a couple of minutes!

Begin by placing your tongue behind your front teeth. Now breathe in sharply through your nose to the count of four. Hold your breath to the count of eight, and then slowly and thoroughly exhale through your mouth to a count of seven. Do this four times in a row. For those who border on the excessive side, please note that four times is all that is necessary for transforming results.

Take time to rest/sleep

When our schedules get overly-full, it seems like the first thing we let go of is sleep and/or rest. Even though we are told that the optimum adult requirement for sleep is seven to nine hours each night, how many of us come close to that on a good day, let alone when there is just too much to do? Instead of going to bed at a reasonable hour, what do we typically do? We throw in another load of laundry, balance the checkbook, finish the report, bake brownies for the next day, get on the computer, or numb out with mindless television. Our need for bed rest gets put on the back burner and the consequences are not only felt by us, but by those around us as well.

When we are overly-tired, everything feels like an effort. And because our bodies lack energy, we often look for some quick fix to re-energize us— sugar, caffeine, drugs, prescription and otherwise, even alcohol. Just look at the recent popularity of hyper-sugared, hyper-caffeinated, "energy" drinks! Their increase in sales is symptomatic of how exhausted we are as a society, and how frequently we look for *something* to get us through the day, event, program, or task. The problem is, most of these quick fixes ultimately backfire on us. The same things we use to keep us alert during the day, keep us up at night, thus compounding our problems the following day, and contributing to a downward spiral.

Nothing distorts our perception of reality more than fatigue. When we don't get enough rest, even the smallest things can mushroom out of control. Our feelings get easily hurt, we can quickly fly into a rage, and/ or our perspective can become bleak, negative, and even hopeless. If that were not bad enough, being chronically sleep-deprived increases our risk for cardiovascular disease, diabetes, and obesity. Yet, a huge population of us suffers from periodic or chronic insomnia. How can we address this dilemma?

To begin with, we must resist making pharmaceuticals our first choice. Instead of reaching, once again, for the quick fix, why not try something different? It only takes a few lifestyle changes to immensely improve our chances for getting the rest we need. These suggestions really work.

- Do not drink caffeine after 2 p.m. This does not simply refer to coffee or tea; most soft drinks are loaded with caffeine, as is chocolate. Try cutting these things out for a week and see what happens. Be willing to be pleasantly surprised!
- Put yourself in the right place at the right time. In other words, resist falling asleep on the couch. And instead of folding laundry,

paying bills, redoing your resume, or making a phone call that is certain to rev you up at 10:30 at night, go to bed! In fact, it is very helpful to go to bed around the same time every night, provided it is a reasonable hour.

- Do not watch television, especially the news, right before trying to sleep. Read something instead, preferably something on the calming side.
- If you are worried about a particular issue, take a few minutes to write about it before going to bed. Putting it down on paper helps to get it out of your head.
- Try some homeopathic remedies such as calcium with magnesium, valerian root, melatonin, herbal teas, or warm milk with turmeric, honey, and ginger.
- Listen to a meditation tape, do a few gentle yoga stretches, or take a hot bath before retiring.
- Watch your alcohol intake. Like certain medications, alcohol can disrupt a good night's sleep.
- Get up on time.

After trying all of these, if you still can't sleep, consider seeing a professional. It is important to remember, however, that sleeping prescriptions are not meant as a way of life, but only as a temporary bridge.

It's not just sleep that we are speaking of here, but also the importance of rest and intentional downtime. Huge benefits can be derived by incorporating little "me-breaks" throughout our busy days. These are small periods of time in which we cease all busyness and just

Nothing distorts our
perception of reality
more than fatigue.

take a break! We can put our feet up either in the office or at home with a good cup of herbal tea; we can periodically shut our door and close our eyes for five or ten minutes; or we could practice our centering breath.

The truth is, stress that is left unattended will always build and pick up speed. It becomes like a snowball rolling downhill, quickly increasing in size and intensity. However, even the smallest amount of "time-out" can disarm it by breaking its destructive cycles. Even if our first response to taking time for ourselves is to feel guilty, we just have to do it anyway.

Probably the most important time to schedule a small "me-break" is between work and home. If our usual custom is to race from one into the other, we might try to take a few moments on either end to become still and centered. Just a few minutes sitting quietly in the car, or maybe taking a five minute brisk walk, will change the dynamics in powerful and positive ways. This cannot be overemphasized.

Watch your intake of food and drink

In many ways, our eating and drinking habits contribute to our out-of-balance lifestyles, especially if we have difficulty with moderation. We finish a job or a task and can't wait to reward ourselves with junk food or with a few too many drinks. We run out of steam and grab another cup of java. We suffer a loss or disappointment and console ourselves with ice cream or fast food. Our emotions get stirred and we fuel them even more by feeding sugar to our anger, giving caffeine to our anxiety, adding alcohol to our despair. Or we go to the other extreme and punish ourselves with starvation or deprivation.

It is a fact that diabetes and hypoglycemia are prevalent in our society. For many of us, our blood sugars can run high or low, influencing sudden mood swings and causing us to feel shaky, cranky, nervous, fatigued and/or depressed. And every time we reach for the wrong thing to give us relief or to re-energize us (more sugar, alcohol, junk food, caffeine), we exacerbate the situation. We may alleviate our symptoms momentarily, but we contribute to the long-term problem and the downward spiral continues.

Remember, our primary goal right now is just to get a little more balance in our lives. We can't possibly do this without taking better care of ourselves. So with that thought in mind, and being *curious not critical*, let's take just a moment to examine our own personal relationship with food. We don't need to make this more complicated than it needs to be. In fact, where food or drink is concerned, there are really just two questions to consider:

- Am I abusing my body in any way by how and what I eat or don't eat, drink or over-drink?
- Do my eating or drinking habits bring me closer or further away from the man/woman I want to be?

Depending on your answers, you might want to seek further information/assistance. At the same time, the following suggestions will help you incorporate some healthier habits, while continuing to increase your awareness.

- Know what you are going to eat for the day. In other words, plan ahead. Don't skip breakfast. Stick to a regular meal schedule.
- Limit or avoid fast food completely.
- Don't eat after 8:30 p.m.
- Drink water rather than soda. Not only are most soft drinks loaded with caffeine, but the diet drinks also contain chemicals that make us feel hungrier over time, rather than satisfied.
- Make a decision where NOT to eat: in the car, in front of the television, at the computer, standing at the kitchen counter, running out the door, or in bed. Instead, eat sitting at the table, preferably with some music, candles, and/or companions.
- When it comes to alcohol consumption, be aware of when, why, and how much.

Just one small change in any of our habits is capable of setting off a positive chain reaction, promoting remarkable long-term results for the better.

Move a muscle

If physical balance and well-being are what we want, exercise is essential! This is true for many reasons:

- Exercise is a natural antidote to anxiety, depression, anger, unconscious eating, and/or acting out.
- It stimulates endorphins, thereby lifting our mood and changing our perspective.

- Exercise makes us stronger and helps us to look better, which, in turn, increases our self-esteem and self-confidence.
- Exercise can break our tendency to get caught up and stuck in obsessive or negative thinking. *Move a muscle; change a thought!*

Still, despite all of these benefits, many of us will want to skip right over this section. Our first thoughts may be, "I hate to exercise," or "Who has time for that?" or "I would if I could but my back, shoulder, arm, knee won't allow it." Yes, to be sure, we can find any number of excuses to stay on the couch or in the chair.

Perhaps we don't understand that exercise is not an all or nothing proposition. It is not necessary for us to run a marathon or even join a gym! We don't have to take up skiing or climb a mountain. We only need to find some way to move our body and get our heart pumping. If it moves, we must move it because if we don't, we will eventually lose it. That really is the truth.

How, then, do we begin?

- Think big but start small. Develop a future vision of your physical self. Where do you want to be in a month, six months, or in a year? Do you want to fit into a certain outfit, have stronger bones, greater muscle tone, more confidence, or increased self-esteem? Envision the end results but begin with baby-steps.
- Put your resistance or lack of confidence on the back burner. This does not need to be like other attempts which may not have worked for you. Be willing to start anew and to be surprised.

- Try to think of something physical that you enjoy doing, such as walking, running, biking, bowling, tai chi, yoga, dancing, taking a hike. If you can't think of anything you enjoy, consider something you can tolerate.

- Put a little "skin" in the game. Buy a walking/jogging outfit or a new pair of sneakers, join a gym or an indoor pool, sign up for aerobic dance, a kick-boxing class, or dance lessons. Investing a bit of money can be great motivation for suiting up and showing up.

- Plan and schedule your exercise. You will probably need to remove something else from the "outgoing energy" side of your Time Energy Awareness (T.E.A.) chart in order to fit exercise on the opposite column. Plan on it, write it down, schedule it, commit to specific days and times, and then show up for yourself.

- Change your thought-talk regarding exercise. Instead of "I have to...," start thinking, "I want to...." Actually, this little change in attitude is helpful for every change you *want* to make!

- Find ways to become accountable. Walk or ride a bike with friends who are dependable, meet a reliable person at the gym, or hire a personal trainer or life coach who can help you help yourself.

- Understand the three-week rule. With any new behavior, the first three weeks are the hardest. If you can persevere for this period of time, exercise will begin to become a habit, and soon you won't feel right without it.

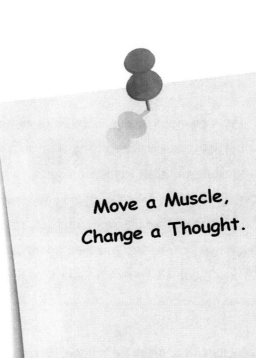

Move a Muscle,
Change a Thought.

Plan your work; work your plan

Chances are, when you made the original list of what you do in a day, you discovered that a lot of your time is consumed in non-productive or perhaps non-fulfilling ways. Maybe your list revealed that you spend hours on the Internet or in front of the television. Perhaps you became aware of spending an inordinate amount of time being the "go-to" person for everyone else.

Or maybe a lot of your energy is consumed by worrying about what needs to be done rather than actually doing it! This is where it really pays to plan your work and work your plan. In fact, it might be a good thing to use a few of those quiet morning moments to consider what really has to be done in the day ahead. Take the time to actually come up with a game plan. Write it down, make a list, and then prioritize that list. It can be helpful to put your list on a 3-by-5 card, keep it handy, and check things off as they are accomplished.

For the bigger jobs, it helps to break them into daily bite-size pieces. For instance, we all know that it would be impossible to pick up a board that was 365 feet long. But if it were broken up into one-foot sections, it could be easily managed. A book is written one page at a time; a house is built one nail at a time, and so forth. This is what we are called to do with our larger projects.

There are many tricks to managing time better. In fact, whole books have been written on the subject. But for right now, we could start in a couple of easy ways. We can make a decision to limit interruptions and distractions in order to tend to business. We could decide to spend less time "vegging-out." We could plan specific days/times to do specific things; for instance, cooking for the week ahead on a weekend afternoon, designating a particular time for opening and paying bills, committing to a specific day to do laundry or take care of the yard. If we can schedule certain times to do certain chores, they won't feel as if they are always hanging over our heads. This alleviates more stress than we can imagine.

Making a game plan also gives us an opportunity to incorporate me-time into the day. Truthfully, we can't keep giving <u>of</u> ourselves without giving <u>to</u> ourselves. And this is not about putting oneself first at the expense of others. It is about *including* ourselves; in other words, "me, too!"

Why is it that we have such difficulty doing this? Perhaps taking care of oneself was never modeled for us. Maybe we were taught from an early age to be caretakers for everyone else, even learning self-sacrifice to such a degree that we often feel spiritually, physically, and emotionally bankrupt as a result. Well, today is a new day and it is time we began refilling our own well; because, let's be very clear—nobody else is going to do this for us!

Self-care always begins with a decision; a decision that we are worth having our own needs taken care of. And even if we don't feel worthy right now, we can still "act as if" by taking some of the following suggestions:

- Come home from work at a reasonable hour.
- Keep the bedroom uncluttered and the bed made.
- Take mini breaks throughout the day.

- Lower unrealistic self-expectations, i.e., let go of perfectionism.
- Get rid of the "shoulds."
- Make healthy food choices.
- Turn the computer or television off at a reasonable time.
- Read inspirational material.
- Go to bed on time.
- Take good care of teeth, skin, eyes, and hair.
- Get a massage, facial, pedicure, manicure.
- Go to the movies, a ballgame, or other fun events with friends.
- Laugh whenever possible.

Incorporating some of these self-care practices will be a real stretch for many of us. But, hopefully, we are ready to be stretched.

Exercise 4: Refill the Well

Taking into account what you have just read, take another look at your T.E.A. chart from the beginning of this section on Balance. Think about ways in which you can renew, refill, and re-energize yourself. You might start by listing at least ten behaviors which you consider self-nurturing. If you can't think of ten, begin with five! Remember, these should all move you in the direction of personal well-being.

After you've made the list, make a decision to do at least one of these behaviors each day. Every morning, ask yourself: "What one good thing can I do for myself today?" Put it on your list. Then, JUST DO IT!

Just for today,
I will not "should"
all over myself.

Chapter Three: Stay Accountable

By now, we have done several positive things. We have taken an honest look at where our time and energy go. We made a decision to take at least one thing off our never-ending list of things to do each day. We gained some insight regarding what really matters to us. We've looked at several ways to renew and support our physical and emotional well-being. We even made a list of what we consider healthy self-care practices, and committed to doing one good thing for ourselves each day. Wow! That's great! Our awareness is increasing, our stress is reducing, and we are recovering some much-needed energy.

However, the thing about balance that frequently throws us "off balance" is that the center point continually shifts. It can seem as if we just begin to get our feet under us when the playing field changes. Life happens, people surprise, and circumstances fluctuate, often with little or no prior warning. We must pay attention to this tendency and make the necessary adjustments when need be. One thing is for certain:

If we don't continue taking active steps on a daily basis towards living a more balanced and serene lifestyle, we will be insidiously pulled back into feeling overextended, overwhelmed, overly-busy, and out of balance.

Bearing in mind that balance and self-care go absolutely hand in hand, and that they require our active participation every day, the best way to approach the changes we need and *want* to make is to...

Start somewhere

According to Mark Twain, "The secret of getting ahead is getting started. The secret of getting started is breaking complex overwhelming tasks into small manageable tasks, and then starting on the first one." It doesn't matter where or how we begin to incorporate balance/self-care in our life—as long as we do! This is not an endeavor that can be put off indefinitely. We need to stop conning ourselves into thinking that somewhere down the line our life is suddenly going to offer all these opportunities to take better care of ourselves. It won't. So...

Keep it simple

Some changes will be easier to implement than others. If we begin with the more attainable goals, we help to set ourselves up for success. For example, we could start the ball rolling by taking something off our huge list of "things to do" that is easily removable. Then, we can pick a self-care or balance action that resonates with us, one that fits our schedule and is doable; one we are likely to stick with. Success begets success. It is also helpful for us to...

Stay right-sized

Our movement into balance and self-care won't happen overnight; it will be a gradual, incremental journey. And while it is important to have *reasonable* self-expectations, we must guard against setting the bar so high that we are bound to fail. We have undoubtedly done this in the past, and it always leads to self-sabotage. We don't have to do that this time, provided we stay right-sized with what we *expect* we can change. We also increase our chances for success when we....

Identify a "how" for every "what"

While certainly we need to know *what* changes to make, it is of equal importance to know *how* to implement them. We can't just say, "I'm going to exercise an hour every day, make healthy food choices, and take me-time." These are all worthy goals to be sure, but they will not happen until we know how to bring them forth. In other words, what are we willing to take off our plate in order to fit in something new? What is our game plan for instituting these new self-care practices? What do we need to do and when and how can we do it?

In order to maintain any lifestyle change over the long haul, we must really take a look at our schedules and figure out how these new goals can survive. Once again, we want to set ourselves up for success. Along this line, it is also helpful to....

Be accountable

Our chances of attaining and maintaining our balance goals increase significantly when the accountability factor is present. If we doubt that, we might want to review our own personal history of "going it alone." How well has it worked? If the answer is, "not very well," then it is imperative to find ways to keep ourselves accountable, while being supported and encouraged along the way. We all need people who believe in us and who will help us check up on ourselves, even if it's somebody who will give us a kick in the butt every now and then just to let us know they are still behind us!

There are several ways to get support and stay accountable at the same time. We can join an ongoing group. Just look at the success rate of groups like Weight Watchers or 12-step programs. It's not just the fellowship that makes these programs successful; it is also the accountability factor. We could sign up for classes where we will be expected to show up! Or we could find a buddy or two to take this journey with us. In fact, this book and the work in it are perfect to do with a close friend or even in a group. Another great way to stay accountable is to...

Acknowledge successes

Finding creative ways to acknowledge and record successes helps us become our own cheerleader and coach combined. There are many ways to go about this. We could put a big X on the calendar every time we show up for our intention to exercise. We could even put it in a bold color to see it easily, thus encouraging us to keep going. We could use gold stars to keep track of our progress in other areas, such as getting enough rest, eating well, or taking mini breaks throughout the day. We could even design our own accountability chart specific to our personal goals, and then fill it in at the end of each day. This could include writing down what we eat, when we exercise, what one good thing we did for ourselves that day, or how well we honored "what really matters."

None of us needs to remain frantic, frazzled, or frenzied for one more day! We really don't. We have choices, even though they may not be easy to make or to maintain. But if we can be willing to take the risk to try some different dance steps, and then to persevere with our efforts, we will definitely notice some positive results. Not only will we feel and look better, but we will also be able to more easily achieve some of our other goals. We need to do this; we *want* to do this. As the saying goes, "What I do with today is important because I am exchanging a day of my life for it."

So before racing into the next chapter, take some time RIGHT NOW to think about and begin to apply what you have learned thus far. Make a decision to move through and beyond any left-over resistance and to make some good, solid commitments toward your own desires for balance and self-care. Remember: The more willing you can be to take the suggestions put forth, the greater your chances of achieving success. This is where balance begins. And, excuse the redundancy, but if not now, when?

<u>Reader Commitment for Greater Balance</u>

In order to begin restoring balance in my life, I commit to the following:

_____

_____

_____

Today's Date: _____

Notes on Part One

Part Two:
Achieve Emotional Freedom

We are now going to look at ways to recover another kind of energy—the emotional energy we waste every time we allow our thoughts and emotions to govern our moods and to rule the day, especially when they gravitate towards and attach themselves to the negative.

It is as if we get up in the morning and commence at once to fill an imaginary backpack with all kinds of emotional baggage. Take worry for instance. We can pick it up in a nanosecond regarding practically any topic. We worry about things that have already happened and things that might or might not happen in the future. We worry about what other people are doing or not doing; thinking, or not thinking. We "awfulize" and "catastrophize"—about our children, our health, our jobs, our money, our partners, or our lack of the same. Often, we can't even put a finger on what we're so concerned about; we just live with a pervasive and exhausting sense of generalized anxiety.

We also weigh ourselves down with resentments, regrets, and unmet expectations. Carrying shame, remorse, and guilt wears us out even more. Sometimes our emotional heaviness is the result of trying to keep painful memories and hurtful feelings at bay. In the past, we may have not known how to appropriately express or deal with these difficult emotions, so we ended up stuffing, suppressing, denying, distorting, and/or trying to outrun them instead; all of which adds to our emotional baggage.

And what about the biggest drain of all on our enthusiasm and emotional energy—constantly finding fault with ourselves? Self-deprecating thought-talk can spring up out of nowhere, and often, to reinforce our inner distortion that we are not quite good enough. We don't look good enough, act good enough, do enough, have enough, or be enough. We think that we should have, or shouldn't have; could have, or might have. We compare ourselves and our circumstances with others and we always come out on the short end. It's exhausting!

Modern technology further exacerbates our lack of emotional freedom. Seldom do we have downtime anymore, or silence, or periods in which to reflect, regroup, or to process the day's events and our ensuing emotions. Anybody can intrude upon our space at any time. And, of course, someone is always looking for us, needing something.

Yes, we are on emotional overload and it is not getting better on its own. It really is time to make some pivotal changes. We have already incorporated some new practices to increase balance. Now let's go one step further, and learn how to achieve some emotional freedom. This is going to involve our willingness to let go, let go, and let go even more. And although it may be challenging at first, the more emotional energy we are able to recover and reclaim, the more we will have to put into "what really matters."

The most universal misuse
of our emotional and
mental energies is this:
telling ourselves, in one
way or another, that we're
not good enough.

Chapter Four: Learn How to Let Go

So why are we so often distracted, preoccupied, overwhelmed, anxious, or just plain *heavy-hearted*? How did we get in the habit of picking up all of this emotional baggage in the first place?

There is both a simple answer and a more complex one to these questions. The deeper matter has to do with the fact that "we are who we are for reasons, most of them long past." And while we are not going to go into detail regarding this concept at this time, it is important to understand that much of what emotionally exhausts us comes from somewhere on the road behind us. In other words, our tendency to be emotionally burdened is due to the many misconceptions that we have picked up along the way and under which we continue to labor. These are misconstrued ideas and life-views that are, indeed, distorted and unreal. And depending upon our personal history, individual upbringing, and the people and circumstances of our lives, we all have some very predictable ones. Chances are that we aren't really *aware* of these underlying misconceptions, but we live our lives in accordance with them nonetheless. And they wear us out like practically nothing else.

Some of the universal ones include:

- I need to get them before they get me.
- What happened in the past shouldn't bother me today.
- There is not enough to go around.
- Self-care is for those who have the time and money.

- I should be able to do it myself.
- It is a sign of weakness to ask for help.
- There are certain things that should *never* be shared.
- My way is the right way.
- It's my job to take care of *everything*.

And, of course, the biggest misconception of them all:

- I am not worthy or good enough or enough.

It is this last distortion that sets us up for all kinds of emotional turmoil. And although we are not going to go into depth right now regarding the "itty bitty shi..y committee" that lives in our heads, we really need to be aware that a tremendous amount of our emotional energy is siphoned off each time we find fault with ourselves. We are also not going to address those other misconceptions listed at this time; at least not head-on. Instead, we are going to deal with some of their energy-draining *side-effects* which are more obvious. We can't get to the underlying issues without first freeing up some of this more easily-accessible emotional energy.

So what does all of this mean? Well, simply put, we are driven and drained by many underlying issues which we can't begin to address without first freeing up the emotional energy we expend in more apparent ways. In this section of the book, we will address those things that we become obviously attached to which do not support health, harmony, and wholeness. This does not only refer to relationships, jobs, and the like, but also to self-defeating emotions, thoughts, and attitudes which inwardly distract and deplete us; things like resentments, regrets, remorse, and worry, to name a few.

We have held on to a lot of these things, especially this emotional baggage, long after it would be prudent to let go. Why is this? Why have we failed to let go even when we know we would be better off doing so? Well, one reason is because we aren't always clear about *what* we need to let go of, and we don't really understand *how* to let go. We think that it should be a quick fix, an easy do. Whether person, thing, attitude, or habit, we are under the mistaken belief that once we identify what we consider to be the source of our emotional discomfort, we should instantly have the wherewithal to be rid of it. Yet, how often does this actually happen? Our history would undoubtedly reveal that it is seldom.

The reason for this is because letting go is a *process,* not a decision. The decision is necessary for sure, as it moves us into the process. But the process itself consists of a *series* of actions, changes, or functions necessary to bring about the freedom that we seek. Understanding this process is how we begin to lighten our emotional load.

This is what the process of letting go involves:

- Letting go begins with awareness. We can't let go of anything until we absolutely recognize that we need to.
- This awareness often originates out of a sense of intense discomfort or pain.
- There is normally a period of time between our initial awareness and our subsequent ability to take the action necessary to let go.

- Letting go generally involves a final surrender, a last "gasp," a real decision to open our fists and just release what we tightly clench.
- Letting go requires taking new steps with which we are seldom familiar or comfortable.
- Letting go does not involve a struggle.

Let's look at these points more closely.

Strange as it may seem, the first step of the letting go process—awareness—is often the most difficult. This is primarily because, when we are feeling stuck or in emotional turmoil, our first inclination can be to point the finger. We blame him, her, a career, a problematic situation, our children, financial insecurity, or an unjust circumstance. While certainly any of these are capable of exhausting us and causing some real problems, our real difficulties are more often related to those underlying attitudes, assumptions, and thoughts which lie just beneath the surface of our consciousness. Our failure to understand this causes us to spin our wheels like practically nothing else.

The good news is, emotional discomfort can be a great teacher. When the pain gets great enough, we are often willing to look at what we *really* need to get rid of. That said, this is seldom a straight process as our awareness can be immediately followed by all kinds of rationalization, self-will, resistance, magical thinking, or denial. These self-saboteurs jump right in to try and convince us that maybe we were premature, perhaps we can wait a little longer, that there is no need to rush.

For instance, we may know in our hearts that it is time to leave a relationship, a job, or to change a bad habit, for weeks or months before being ready or willing to actually do it. Similarly, we may recognize that we are carrying around resentments, regrets, or unrealistic expectations long before we are prepared to let them go. After all, we are familiar with those things we cling to, and we worry about what would replace them if we actually did let them go. Besides, we think, bad breath is better than no breath!

This "betwixt and between" period is like living in a hallway of "divine discomfort." We know at some level that we need to let go, but we're not quite ready to do so yet. As bad as it might feel, this discomfort is often necessary to eventually move us into doing what we need to do. To this end, our unease is a gift.

Probably the most critical piece of information regarding letting go is that it *does not involve a struggle.* That's right; no struggle necessary. Think about it. Struggle involves energy. But is the energy being used to let go? Or are our efforts more involved in holding on? Consider the following illustration.

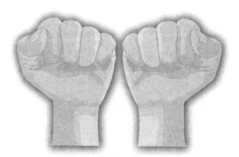

Holding On   Letting Go

Which act requires the energy?

If we are struggling
to let go, chances are that
we are holding on instead.

How, then, do we avoid the struggle? The answer is simple and it works in all cases.

When it comes to letting go, rather than put our energy and attention on what we wish to leave behind or to be rid of, we shift our focus. We turn away from the very conditions that create discomfort and distress, and place our attention instead on where we want to go. Rather than exhaust ourselves in the distraction and struggle of trying to become free of anything—a person, attitude, habit, or behavior—we take our attention off the "problem" and use that same energy to walk purposefully into the "solution"; down a different path, one that is uniquely ours.

We often don't become willing to make this shift without benefit of a final surrender. This is when we really embrace the fact that, yes, it is time to give it up, get rid of it, let it go, and move on. This stage usually arrives when we are sick and tired of being sick and tired! When in our hearts and minds, we become *willing to be different;* open to having our lives change for the better. Once we do, things usually happen quickly, often in ways we never could have imagined. Doors fly open; new opportunities present themselves; negative behaviors and attitudes are replaced by positive ones. And we wonder why we took so darn long to let go in the first place.

Another reason we might find ourselves "struggling" to let go is because we so often confuse the process of letting go with our need to heal. This confusion has been responsible for many of our past difficulties. When heartbreak, losses, and abuses are involved, it is not possible to let go of the accompanying pain. *Grief must be healed instead.* This is such an important topic, and is at the root of so much of our driven-ness and distress, that the entire sequel to this book, *The Busy Person's Guide to Inner Healing,* has been written to address this issue.

For now, however, let's just keep it simple by finding ways to reduce the emotional energy we waste in more recognizable behaviors.

We cannot, under
any circumstances,
let go of what must
be healed instead.

Chapter Five: Not to Worry

So here we are, with our imaginary backpacks loaded to the rim, filled with all kinds of emotional baggage—worry, disappointments, regrets, anxiety, resentments, feelings of "less-than," comparisons, and other energy-drainers. We pick these up without even giving it any thought; a habit that has resulted in our walking around with a weight upon our shoulders and heaviness within our hearts. We want and need to lighten up. But, prior to now, we haven't had any directions! Now we do, and a good place to begin putting them into action is by looking at our ever-present tendency to worry.

Worry is prevalent in our society. In fact, some of us are so accustomed to worrying that we don't feel right if we're not. Perhaps we can identify with the woman who was driving down the highway completely preoccupied with worrisome thoughts. Distracted by something in the road, she briefly forgot what she was worried about. Immediately, she became consumed with anxiety because she couldn't remember her worry! To say that we're attached to the habit of worrying is not completely far-fetched. Think about how often the word "worry" shows up in our daily conversation, let alone our daily thoughts. In fact, some of us think it is part of our job description, that if we're not worrying, we're not doing anything constructive about the situation! Nothing could be further from the truth.

So what exactly are we worried about? If it involves one of our children, what are our specific concerns? Are we worried that they are not making the choices we want them to? Are we concerned that they are using drugs or alcohol or that they might? Do we worry about the friends they are making or not making?

If we are losing sleep over our finances, do we actually know our bottom line? Have we been putting our head in the sand for such a long period of time that we are confused about what the reality is? Could we be unduly alarmed?

If we are worried about a health issue, a relationship, or an upcoming event, do we know what the precise nature of our worry is? Remember, we can't let go of anything without first identifying exactly what it is that we are dealing with.

The following story is taken from my first book, *The Joy is in the Journey: A Woman's Guide through Crisis and Change*. It so aptly depicts the process necessary to let go, I couldn't resist using it in this book as well.

My son was not quite three when I was diagnosed with breast cancer. As anyone might imagine, this was certainly a cause for great concern on my part. A year later, I became even more worried when a routine bone scan revealed something "unusual." The doctors didn't think it was consistent with cancer, yet they couldn't tell me what it was.

I became obsessed with the negative possibilities. I lost sleep, and couldn't eat. Totally preoccupied with my "concern," I spent many hours consumed by it, to the point of poking and feeling the suspicious area trying to determine abnormalities. One day, I even went so far as to take out my old college Anatomy and Physiology book. There I was, sitting at the dining room table with Dr. Susan Love's book on breast cancer in one hand and the Anatomy book in the other. At the same time, my young son was in the other room watching a National Geographic special on television. He kept interrupting by calling, "Mommy! Mommy! Come see."

"In a minute, Robert," I replied. "I'm busy right now."

"But hurry, Mommy!" he implored.

At this point I was so consumed with my worry that I had no patience for anything else.

"Not now!" I yelled.

Wounded by my harsh reply, my son began to cry. He walked slowly toward me, with tears streaming down his precious face.

"But Mommy, you're missing all the beautiful butterflies!"

I could not have had a greater moment of truth if somebody had hit me over the head with a baseball bat. In that one instant, I realized the enormous waste of energy created by my worrying. Not only was it serving no good purpose, but it was also robbing me of the capacity to be present to anyone or anything else.

My son helped me learn an important lesson that day. When it comes to worry, once we have identified the worrying source, we must then ask ourselves an important question:

"Is there anything I can do *right now* to help elicit a positive outcome in this regard?"

If the answer is yes, we must take the action it requires in a timely way. This might involve making a doctor's appointment, seeing a lawyer, sending out a resume, writing a letter, addressing a personal boundary, doing some research, meeting with a financial advisor, building a support system, or joining a group. If there is *anything* we can do to move in the direction of a positive outcome, we must stop procrastinating and just do it!

In cases where there is absolutely nothing more to be done, when we have taken whatever steps we could to get positive results, there are additional tools we can use to reinforce our efforts at letting go.

Practice mind-shifting

Great relief from our worrying thoughts is only a mental shift away. This is about making a conscious decision to switch our internal radio station from W.O.E. to W.O.W. In other words, we stop thinking and obsessing about the problem (over which we have done everything possible, right?), and place our attention on some positive thought instead; we move out of "awfulizing" and focus on things like love, nature, gratitude, a past joyful experience, even looking forward to a great meal or good cup of tea. This will not be an easy move for those of us who have spent years in the habit of worrying. However, with practice, relief will come. And remember, shifting the focus never involves a struggle.

Turn it over

Finding creative ways to let go, or to "turn it over," is also helpful in this regard. We can get relief by writing down what we're worried about, checking that we have done everything possible at this moment in time, and then making a conscious decision to let our worry go. We could take this one step further by placing the written piece in some type of receptacle, such as a "God-box" of our own creation. Even if we don't consider ourselves as having any kind of faith, we can still get great relief from the physical act of transferring the worry from our head, onto the paper, and into some container. This is a wonderful ritual to use with children who tend to worry as well.

Pay attention to the butterflies

We are only victims to our habit of worrying if we choose to be. No matter how familiar worrying might be to us, today we have a choice. We can pick up our concerns as if they were essential, hold them close to us, and allow them to drain our energy and preempt everything wonderful in our lives. OR... we can make a conscious decision to pay attention to the beautiful "butterflies" which are present somewhere. We need not look far to find *something* for which to be grateful. This is where we must put our focus. As we do, we can affirm to ourselves that, "all will be well."

Exercise 5: Let Go of Worry

Take a few minutes to think about your most pressing concerns. Are you worried about something specific, or is it more of a generalized anxiety? Spend some time journaling to see if you can uncover the root of your anxiety. The more specific you can be, the greater will be your chances of letting it go.

Once you have identified the exact nature of your concern, ask yourself: "Is there anything I can do *right now* to affect a positive outcome with this? If the answer is yes, make a commitment to do whatever needs to be done. Then take the necessary action—sooner rather than later!

If the answer is no and there is nothing more that can be done, find a way to symbolically release what you are worried about. Write down whatever concerns you and place it in a God-box or some other receptacle of your own making; share your worries with a good friend, preferably one who will not add fuel to the fire; or employ your new mind-shifting technique. Whenever the worry enters your mind, immediately think of something more positive. In fact, this might be a good time to sit down and make a gratitude list. There is always something good going on when we look for it. All of this will become easier over time and with consistent practice.

Chapter Six: Release Resentment and Anger

Two additional emotions that can be extremely problematic are those of anger and resentment. We seethe with one and hold fast to the other. Both weigh us down tremendously. Why, then, do we keep picking them up and continuing to carry them?

One reason is that many of us just don't know how to appropriately be angry. When this emotion comes up, it can frighten us, or we can judge our feeling as being wrong or bad. Often, we have no tools for expressing our anger in reasonable and healthy ways. We've just never been taught. So, instead, we deny, stuff, minimize, or explode with it, none of which works well for us or those around us.

All of our emotions and feelings have value. They have been given to us for a reason. They are our teachers, here to increase our understanding of ourselves and others. Anger, for instance, can be a justified and appropriate response to injustice, foul play, being treated badly, having our boundaries violated, feeling taken advantage of, and the like. When life isn't fair, or we are not treated well, it's normal to feel angry.

Anger can also be a smokescreen, a cover-up for something deeper. Frequently, it is our first line of defense against feeling hurt or slighted. We prefer anger to sadness because we get some energy from it. It can even work for us at times. Many a house or garage has been cleaned from top to bottom in an angry tirade!

Sometimes anger is part of an inner grieving process of which we may or may not be aware. Or it could be that something in our present circumstances has triggered some old emotional baggage that has not yet been healed. And, of course, anger often comes to tell us that we are way off our personal balance beam.

Still, if we were to really look closely, we would undoubtedly find that most of our anger gets its energy from fear. That's right; we get angry when we're afraid; afraid that we're not going to get what we need, want, or deserve; afraid that we are going to lose something that we have; afraid that we are somehow being taken advantage of or not given our fair share of attention, money, prestige, promotions, even our fair share of the road! We're afraid that we are being left out, not seen or heard, undermined, or dismissed. These underlying fears, many of them originating a long time ago, are almost too many to mention! How then, can we even begin to deal with the anger that they arouse—and to deal with it before doing harm to somebody else or to ourselves?

We need to dis-empower the anger as quickly as possible; to take the damaging energy out of it. And there are several ways to go about this. Let's look at a few.

Stop judging your feelings

In many cases, our feelings, in and of themselves, don't cause the greatest problem. Instead, it is our JUDGMENT of our feelings that wipes us out. We perceive emotional responses such as anger as somehow being wrong. So when we have this feeling, we mentally and emotionally beat ourselves up just for having the feeling! This takes more of our energy than anything else. In fact, our tendency to judge our feelings is one of our biggest self-saboteurs. We know this is true.

In reality, feelings are never good or bad, right or wrong. They are simply feelings. So part of the work we are called upon to do, is to give ourselves permission to feel all of them, even those feelings we deem "negative." This is called "acceptance" and it is at the opposite end of the spectrum of judgment.

Once we stop fighting with ourselves for simply feeling, we are much more able to learn something from our emotional responses; to listen to what they have to tell us. So when a "negative" feeling such as anger rears its not-so-pretty head, instead of reacting, stuffing, denying, judging, or trying to outrun it, we can instead sit down, pull up a chair, and invite this "anger" to come on in and have a conversation with us. Rather than take our feelings at face value, we learn to look them in the eye, ask some honest questions, and give some honest answers. This is how we begin to uncover some very valuable information. It is all part of the process.

Respond, don't react

There is a big difference between responding and reacting. Chances are that, in the past, we've *reacted* to our angry feelings in ways that haven't been the best; times in which everyone involved has paid a hefty price, including ourselves. So when this emotion comes screaming to the forefront of our feelings, before saying or doing something we will ultimately regret, or damaging our own emotional well-being, we can choose to *respond* instead by doing one of the following:

- We can quickly remove ourselves from the situation.
- We can zip it up for the moment, practicing "restraint of tongue."
- We can go out for a walk or run.
- We can find a "safe" person with whom we can vent/share how we feel.
- We can get our anger out in the written word by journaling.
- We can pound a pillow, throw some hoops, or scrub a floor.
- We can remind ourselves that to act out with anger or rage never makes us or anyone else feel good, or solves the problem.
- We can practice our centering breath, over and over and over again.

Our immediate goal is to quiet ourselves down a bit in order to move back into a more rational and reasonable state of being. We can then take a mini-inventory in order to get at the root of our feelings.

Ask questions

We saw earlier that the only way our feelings can be our teachers is if we stop judging them, learn to pay attention, and look beyond the obvious. So when we are feeling angry, after we have settled down a bit, we need to ask ourselves a few honest questions:

- What's really going on here? Am I out of balance today? Am I hungry or over-tired? Have I been pushing the envelope too much in any given area? And please forgive this author for asking, but for women, could hormones be playing a part?

- Could my angry feelings be related in some way to an underlying fear? What might that fear be? Is this something that comes up for me often?

- Do I tend to be overly-sensitive or over-reactive as a rule, getting angry quickly and often without just cause? In some ways, do I even look for reasons to get my feelings hurt or to feel angry?

- Was reacting with rage a means of communication that was modeled in my family of origin? Could it be that I have never learned appropriate ways of expressing how I feel, and thus get frustrated?

- Has this anger come to tell me that I have been trying to accept something that is clearly unacceptable? Could it be a symptom that the time has come to take some action that I have been avoiding for whatever reason? What would that action look like? Would I feel less angry if I took the action?

It is vital to find healthier ways to express anger because, left unattended, it ultimately ferments into resentment and grudges. And while there is much to be said about these two, none of it is good. Resentments corrode the vessels that carry them. Holding a grudge keeps us emotionally unavailable to the good stuff happening around us. And according to Emmet Fox, "Resentments rot the soul." They not only exhaust us, they also maintain our unhealthy attachment to the source of our contention. Think about it. We are the ones suffering, awake at night, tossing and turning and thinking and fuming. They aren't. And while we can justify our grudges and resentments until the cows come home, there really is no good reason for doing so.

How do we know if we are being negatively affected by these heavy-weights? The most classic symptom of harboring resentment is our tendency to re-feel something that has previously upset or made us angry. It might have even happened years ago, but we keep on re-living it in our mind and re-feeling it in our body. It really is time to let these things go! The following suggestions will help us.

Remove the "to me"

Let's face it: One reason we are so prone to picking up grudges and hanging onto resentments is because we take everything so darn personally. We think the behavior of others is somehow all about us. We believe that their less-than-desirable actions, attitudes, or words were intended to hurt, wound, get even with, or make us feel bad. Even when we don't believe it was intentional, we think they "should have known better."

In reality, they don't. And even though it can feel so deeply personal, *especially* if we have been deceived or betrayed, what they "do" or "don't do" is generally far more related to who <u>they</u> are than who <u>we</u> are. So instead of obsessing over, "Why is he/she doing this *to me*?" we can learn to take the "to me" off the end of that question. It then becomes a whole different animal: "Why is he/she doing this?"

When we remove the supposed intentionality behind another's misguided or wrongful words or actions, we are far less likely to feel hurt, to cop an attitude, or to become preoccupied by obsessively re-playing and re-feeling the perceived wrong. And although chances are good that nothing we might have said or done differently would have changed what happened, we must still be willing to...

Look at our part

We might not want to hear this, but when it comes to dealing with those grudges that we hold so tightly, it is very important to make sure our side of the street is clean. In other words, we must examine our own behavior regarding the circumstances which caused us to feel resentful in the first place. Once again, self-inquiry is essential.

- Did I contribute somehow to what happened? Were some of my own actions, attitudes, or words not what they might have been?
- Do I tend to have unrealistic expectations and then become resentful when they are not fulfilled? (See next section of this chapter for more on this).
- Did I do or say something that might have exacerbated the situation?
- Might I owe somebody an apology or amend as well?

If our resentments are generally of the same variety, only with different players, they probably have more to do with <u>us</u> than with <u>them</u>. We really need to look at this; once again, by being *curious not*

We are not so likely to feel
hurt or resentful if we take
the "to me" off any sentence
that begins with
"Why is he/she doing this?"

critical. After all, we are only gathering information and insight in order to achieve some emotional freedom. To this end, it also can help if we...

Go to the source

If we are feeling resentful toward a particular person over a specific situation, going to the source is usually necessary to achieve resolution. Even if we have been accustomed to talking behind people's backs, reacting with stony silence, or treating them with icy indifference so that they "get the point," now is the time to begin taking steps in a more mature and healthy direction.

Going directly to the source of our discomfort will be a frightening consideration for many of us, especially if we've spent years avoiding any kind of confrontation. In fact, we may not even like that word, believing that confrontation requires anger and outrage. But it doesn't have to be that way at all. Confrontation can simply be a face to face meeting in which we *express* —not yell, scream, or become hysterical over—our feelings about what happened. Or, if we are not ready to meet somebody face to face, we can begin by writing them a letter, one that we can either send or not send. The following format is a good guide to help us learn how to express ourselves whether in the spoken or written word.

"I felt_____, when you_____." It is important to always come from an "I" perspective because the purpose in going to the source is not to point the finger in blame and shame, but to address how somebody else's behavior has made us feel. Besides, the minute we start a sentence off with "You....," whether in person or on paper, the other party immediately shuts down. They can't hear or see another word because they are too busy preparing their defense!

So we begin by expressing our *feelings* about what happened. "*I felt...* (hurt, wounded, angry, betrayed, confused, disappointed, put-down, minimized, excluded, invisible, and so forth)." We can then go on to state the reasons for our feelings, as we see them. "When you... (didn't call, cancelled at the last minute, ignored me, treated me with disrespect, failed to respond to my emails, etc.).

Whether we write and send the letter or go directly to the source, we must understand that everyone involved has a personal viewpoint which is guaranteed to be different from ours. In either case, it is *vital* for us to keep our focus on the event or circumstance that upset us to begin with. It won't help matters for us to drudge up a laundry list of everything else they have ever done that hurt us, or to point out their character defects. Neither one of these would be helpful towards the goal of resolution. So we stay focused on the precipitating event and keep the attention on how a particular situation or behavior made us *feel*. And while our sharing may not be received in the manner in which we intend, that's perfectly okay. We are not responsible for somebody else's reaction; we are simply responsible for speaking our truth and for speaking it kindly. We deserve to have a voice. However, once we do share our feelings, we might also find it necessary to...

Forgive

Just reading that word "forgive" may immediately bring up resistance for many of us. Even so, let's not forget what we are trying to do here. We want to lighten our emotional backpack by getting rid of our resentments. To this end, forgiveness is often necessary. This doesn't imply that what they did was okay. It just means that we don't need to continue wasting OUR energy because of somebody else's behavior. Whether our grudge is against an individual, a group, or even an organization or institution, forgiveness is something we do for ourselves. It is how we take our own power back. It is a way to become re-energized.

Forgiveness begins by making a decision to no longer allow others to have control over how we feel. And then we do whatever we need to do in order to forgive them. Many people use prayer for help in this regard. They pray for those they need to forgive; for their good health and welfare. This is in no way "taking them off the hook." It is taking ourselves out of the role of victim.

If emotional freedom is what we want, we must be willing to go to any lengths to get it. The good news is, after we forgive who or whatever we need to forgive, it then becomes a personal choice whether or not to remain in relationship with those who caused us bad feelings in the first place. If we don't want to, that is perfectly permissible. Even in the case of family members, we can change the frequency and extent to which we are involved. Our next section on Boundaries will help us with this.

If we do decide to maintain a relationship with those who have caused us hurt or emotional distress, we must *really* let bygones be bygones. If we have moments of re-feeling the old stuff, we must remind ourselves that we have let this go, and then bring our head back into where our feet are. This is always easier, of course, when our personal side of the road is in good balance.

Exercise 6: Get Rid of Resentment

Take a few moments to think about any resentments or grudges which you currently harbor. These could be towards a person, a group of people, or even an organization or institution that you feel has "wronged" you in some way. Answer the following:

- Does my holding onto this resentment hurt anyone else but me? Who is losing sleep or raising their blood pressure because of it?
- Am I willing to go to any lengths to be rid of this resentment? What suggestion can I use to help me? Can I depersonalize the behavior by removing the "to me" from the supposed intentionality? Can I go to the source by writing a letter or by using gentle confrontation, always speaking from the "I" perspective?
- Am I willing to pray for the person(s) for whom I hold the resentment? If not, why not? Do I think it would be taking them off the hook? Can I follow that thought through?

- Are my resentments so deep that they may require some additional help? Is this a good time to seek counseling or to speak with a close friend?

Let's not give anybody or anything that much power over our feelings and our moods any longer. The more willing we can become to take the necessary action to rid ourselves of these resentments, the lighter and more energized we will feel. And that really is a guarantee.

Chapter Seven: Let Go and Let Be

Three additional heavy-weights that drain our emotional energy on a daily basis are those of unrealistic expectations (of self, others, and life itself), disappointments, and regrets of a lifetime. Let's look at these three a little more closely.

For the most part, we are probably unaware of the huge role expectations play in our emotional fatigue. We expect things to go a certain way, and when they don't, we feel let down, disillusioned, or that we have somehow failed. We expect our loved ones to know what we want, what we need, and what we are thinking. When they don't, we feel hurt, under-valued, and misunderstood. We project our own standards and desires on others and expect them to act, respond, and behave in ways we want them to or think they should. When they don't, we feel upset, frustrated, and resentful. We do what we think we are supposed to do in order to get the outcomes we want. When life doesn't deliver what we think we deserve, we are disappointed and depressed.

We don't just have these expectations, in many cases, we *justify* having them as well. After all, if we've been working hard, putting in tremendous time and energy, shouldn't we expect some concrete results? A promotion, a contract, a raise, financial security? If we've been involved in a relationship for a length of time, isn't it reasonable to expect the other person to know what we need and how we feel without our having to spell everything out? If we have children, isn't it normal to have expectations of what they should or should not be doing, regardless of their age? And is it wrong to expect things to happen in a reasonable time with a reasonable amount of effort?

While expectations in themselves are not good or bad, what causes the problem is that we so often base our self-esteem or happiness on whether or not they manifest in the ways we expect they should. *When we make our ability to be okay or to be happy contingent on some ultimate outcome or on what somebody else does or doesn't do, we set ourselves up for a huge fall.* This is what they mean when they say: "An expectation is a disappointment in the making."

Of course, some of us go to the other extreme completely, with expectations which are totally negative by nature. We expect things to go wrong, and so they do. We expect bad things will happen to us and our loved ones, and are continually waiting for the other shoe to drop. We are convinced that we will never get what we need or deserve, and that becomes a self-fulfilling prophecy. Oh yes, these types of expectations drain us every bit as much, if not more so, than the others.

No matter how you look at them, expectations are tricky. For one thing, they generally live right beneath the surface of our consciousness. We know they are there without really being aware of them. This gives them a lot of hidden power over our emotional well-being. And because they are capable of dragging us down and dampening our enthusiasm as few other things can, the first order of the day is to wake up and pay attention. We need to start putting two and two together; to become aware of the relationship between how we feel, and what we expect *should* or *should not* happen. The following exercise will help us do this.

87

Exercise 7: Let Go of Expectations

To the best of your ability, make a list of the exact nature of any expectations into which you might knowingly or unconsciously invest a lot of emotional energy. It might help if you think of the word "should"—"I should, he/she should, it should"—as the two go hand in hand. Take your time with this because it really is important.

You can separate these expectations into three individual groups:

- <u>Expectations of others</u>. These include any expectations you might have regarding somebody else's conduct, choices, and decisions.
- <u>Expectations of self</u>. These are expectations placed on personal performance which may be unreasonably high or, in some cases, too low.
- <u>Expectations for particular outcomes</u>. These are expectations of things working out in specific ways; achieving outcomes that you desire.

After making these lists, begin by looking at the expectations you place on others. Ask yourself the following:

- Do I assume that others should automatically know what I want and need without my telling them? How well has this assumption worked in the past?
- Do I expect behavior from others that is not forthcoming? Do I keep telling myself this time will be different? Is this a set-up

for getting my feelings hurt or being disappointed, frustrated, or angry?

- Do I expect others to live up to my personal game plan for their lives? How well has this worked? Do I really think I have the power to change somebody else when it's almost impossible to change myself?
- Can I understand that letting go often simply requires "letting be?"
- What would happen if I could just take my hands off? Would I feel better? Would my relationships improve? Am I willing to give it a try?

When reviewing your list of self-expectations:

- Are my personal expectations right-sized and reasonable or do I set the bar so high that I am continually falling short and feeling less-than?
- Do I expect that I should be able to accomplish more than what is possible in any given time? How might I feel if I took some of the pressure off myself, maybe by removing a few items from my to-do list?
- Are my self-expectations unreasonably low? Am I so afraid of failing that I fail to stretch, take a risk, or try something new?
- Can I see any relationship between self-expectations and perfectionism?

When considering your expectations for particular outcomes:

- Have I taken appropriate and sufficient effort to achieve the outcome I would want?
- Can I understand that I am only responsible for the effort involved and that the results will take care of themselves? And that they might not necessarily materialize the way in which I would like?
- How can I let go of my attachment to the results? Could I turn them over to the Universe? Could this be another occasion to use the God-box, to journal, or to find somebody with whom to speak?

Spend as much time as necessary on this exercise before moving on. This is a big step towards reclaiming our emotional energy!

Dispense with disappointments

Let's be very clear: There is a direct correlation between feeling chronically disappointed and having unmet and unrealized expectations. In other words, when we insist on giving *anything* or *anybody* power over our happiness and well-being, we become vulnerable to an eventual let down. Disappointment can be a catalyst for an emotional slide, as it quickly morphs into self-pity. Self-pity, in turn, takes on a life of its own. Once it gets rolling, it can pick up everything in its path, eventually becoming a huge blob of self-pity /victim /always/never. Talk about heavy!

We need to stop this downward spiral before it gains momentum. After all, life seldom goes the way in which we would like. People don't

Expectations become
a problem when we make
our happiness, well-being,
self-esteem, and serenity
dependent upon their
becoming real.

always respond in the ways we would like them to. And we often fall short of our own goals and ideals. Does this mean we have to feel disillusioned all the time? Of course it doesn't—provided we take some action. And the time to do this is right at the beginning of feeling let down. When disappointment strikes, we must quickly ask ourselves, "Do I really want to go in this direction? Do I need to? What would it take to change my thoughts, RIGHT NOW?"

Our thoughts are what determine our emotional responses. And while we might not be able to instantly change our emotions, we can definitely work on our thoughts. We might enlist some of our new behaviors to help us. We can "move a muscle, change a thought," phone a friend, stop everything and have a cup of tea, journal with our feelings, change our internal radio station, whatever it takes to shift mental directions. Nobody said this was going to be easy. But if we can begin to get a handle on the ways we think, we will be able to guard against falling into these emotional booby traps so easily and frequently.

Release regrets

Regrets are another huge emotional burden that many of us stuff into our daily backpacks. These are different than disappointments. Not only are regrets primarily related to things in the past, but they also have much more to do with us than with others or current circumstances— the opportunities we had but didn't take; the decisions we made that, in hindsight, appear to have been wrong; personal behavior that wasn't what it might have been. We regret the things we did and those we failed to do; the things we said and wish we hadn't; and the things we didn't say that we wish we had. We regret the job we didn't take, the man/woman we did or didn't marry, the investment we failed to make, the house we sold too soon, the money we foolishly squandered, the stories we never read to our children, the vacations we didn't take, the years that passed too quickly.

Even though the majority of our regrets originated on that road behind us, (the one so appropriately called "no longer an option"), we still manage to pick up and carry several through any given day. They are a silent but huge contributor to our feeling lethargic, depressed, and overwhelmed. The deeper and more serious of these regrets may well require the grief work which is addressed in this book's sequel. However, the majority of them may only need recognition, time-limited attention, and a conscious decision to let them go. This is certainly something that we can and must do. The following will show us how.

Exercise 8: Let Go of Regret

Letting go of regrets will take some very focused and intentional effort. This involves designating a time devoted solely to one endeavor; reviewing everything in the past that we wish had not happened, or we wish had happened differently; identifying things that we still long for, maybe something we once had but no longer do, or relationships that we miss because they have changed or are no more.

The best way to go about this is to schedule a period of time in which you won't be disturbed. Settle yourself in, maybe even do a little meditation first, or the centering breath you learned in the section on Balance. Then take pen in hand and write a list of everything in your life that you regret; *everything.* Write as though making a shopping list, item by item. As you do, become aware of any patterns of behavior you may have repeated over and over. This allows you to learn from your past regrets so that you can stop creating more of the same.

After compiling your list, go one step further and *ritualize* the release of them. If you are doing this exercise with others, you may want to share part or all of what you have written. After sharing, you can tear the pages up and ceremoniously throw them into a fireplace or other container to be burned. As they go up in flames, make a conscious decision to offer all of your past regrets up to the Universe, to turn them over, to let them go.

Once you have done this, there is no need to ever dredge up these old regrets again. They are gone! You are rid of them! And if they clamor for your attention, which they most assuredly will at times, don't struggle or fight with them. Just gently remind yourself that you have done this exercise; you have let them go and they can no longer distract you from living your life. Then bring your mental energy back to where your feet are, in today. Congratulate yourself for freeing up space for the new.

Chapter Eight: Move into the Light

Let's not lose sight of our primary purpose for this section of the book: We want to let go of negative emotions that weigh us down and dampen our spirit. We want to free up some energy, become clearer, and enjoy greater emotional balance. After all, we have places to go, changes to make, people to meet, goals to achieve, dreams to manifest! And letting go of our attachment to emotions like worry, resentment, unmet expectations, disappointments, and the regrets of a lifetime will certainly free us up to move in these more positive directions.

Another benefit of lightening up our emotional backpack is that it allows us to address those other concerns which also exhaust our emotional energy; those people, places, and things we are so quick to identify as needing to be let go of.

However, before going further into this area, let's backtrack for just a moment to refresh our memory of the simple (but not easy) formula for letting go.

When it comes to letting go, rather than put our energy and attention on what we wish to leave behind, we shift our focus. We turn away from the very conditions that create discomfort and distress, and place our attention instead on where we want to go. Rather than exhaust ourselves in the distraction and struggle of trying to become free of anything—a person, attitude, habit, or behavior—we take our attention off of the "problem" and use that same energy to walk purposefully into the "solution;" down a different path, one that is uniquely ours.

As it is said, "Where our attention goes, our energy flows." Now, with that thought in mind, let's do one more exercise to apply this formula to what we have learned thus far.

Exercise 9: Continue to Let Go

Take a look at the following and check off those emotional heavy-weights which have proved problematic in the past:

____ Worries

____ Resentments

____ Expectations (self, others, outcomes)

____ Regrets

____ Disappointments

____ Guilt/Shame/Blame

____ Tendency to judge self and others

We have already learned some new tools for dealing with many of these emotional heavy-weights. But, as usual, a little more self-inquiry is always helpful.

- Can you think of any other emotional baggage that you might be picking up and carrying in your imaginary backpack? How long have you been carrying this emotion/attitude/way of relating to the world? Is it a result of a particular circumstance or life experience? Give this some thought and then write about it.

- If you were to head in the opposite direction of your particular "issue," what would that consist of? For example, the opposite of worry is trust/faith. The opposite of resentment is forgiveness. The opposite of disappointment is acceptance as is the opposite of judgment. If you have difficulty with this exercise, use the Internet or a dictionary to look up the opposite of your heavy-weight.

- What action steps can you take, or are you *willing* to take, to move in the opposite direction? For example, if you have fallen into judgment about somebody or something, or are feeling disappointed, those are both symptoms that acceptance is necessary. What can you do to move into acceptance? Can you use ritual? Call somebody to discuss? Address an issue with the appropriate people? Make a list.

The ultimate goal of letting go is emotional freedom and well-being. However, it is important to note that we have been carrying most of these emotional heavy-weights our entire life. Some of them will require the extensive healing work which will be addressed in this book's sequel.

This is especially true for our feelings of guilt, shame, and remorse. We will get to all of these in time. For now, we just need to do what we can do to let go of what we can let go of.

Address outer concerns

We are now ready to address some of our outer circumstances which also create emotional fatigue. These will undoubtedly fall into two different categories.

The first group consists of people and situations we are quick to identify as keeping us stuck, stagnant, unhappy, or unfulfilled. We know who and what they are! These may include a difficult relationship, a soul-sacrificing job, friendships which drain and strain us, or a role or status that hasn't really suited us for a long time. We have held onto some of these relationships and circumstances far longer than we even want to admit. We know the reasons why. They are familiar and the familiar feels safe even when it isn't; the familiar feels right, even though it isn't; the familiar feels easy, when in reality, it is often anything but. We stay with the "known" because we're afraid of the "unknown."

But we are at a point where we are probably becoming more honest with ourselves. We realize that the status quo hasn't been working all that well, perhaps not for years. And there is a part of us that is willing to address our fears and take the necessary steps to let go and move on. We may not know what this will entail, but we have reached bottom with what is.

The more we identify
and let go of emotional
stress, the greater our
chances of being led by
our dreams rather than
driven by our fears.

The second group which we are called upon to let go of is even more challenging than the first. This group involves people and situations that we know we need to release, but we really don't want to. Love relationships that tug at our emotional heartstrings, ones that we have worked hard at maintaining and wanted to keep; adult children that don't require or desire the same degree of attention and parenting; careers and jobs we have loved but which have changed and are no longer the same; roles and statuses that we keep trying to make fit, even though they no longer do. And while it is one thing to detach and let go of people and situations from which, at some level, we want to move on, it is a whole other story when we don't. "Not now," we cry, "I'm just not ready yet!"

When things are near and dear to us, and when the stakes feel high, the fear gremlins can move right in to try and persuade us to maintain the status quo at any cost. "Don't let go," they implore. "What will you be without the relationship, job, role, status _____(fill in the blank)?" These fearful thoughts tell us bad things will happen and good things won't; that we can't live without what we are relinquishing; that we will be less-than, or overwhelmed, or devastated. This makes our letting go process even more difficult.

For the most part, letting go of people, situations, and circumstances that we really don't want to—but know that we must— falls into the category of "things that need to be healed." And, once again, this is a topic and undertaking that we are not quite ready to address right now. But it is important for us to understand that if we are in this place, chances are good that we might need additional help. There are many things that we cannot do by ourselves, and we don't have to. If we are struggling to get out of a difficult situation, we must be willing to do whatever is necessary to help our process, whether it involves therapy, a group process, joining an existing program, or even moving into some kind of acceptance. Maybe a close friend or relative could be helpful. After all, we don't want or need to stay in the murk and mire one minute longer than what is absolutely necessary.

Exercise 10: Redirect Energy

When it comes to those outer circumstances which have been exhausting our emotional energy, and which we are prepared to let go of, the following questions may be helpful. They will definitely require some honest soul searching. Once again, remind yourself that "where your attention goes, your energy flows" and give this exercise the time and thought it requires.

1.) Are you currently struggling in your attempts to let go of a person, situation, or circumstance? If so, is it possible your struggle is really about holding on in some way? What will it take to reach the final surrender?

2.) Have your attempts to let go of a particular person or specific situation caused a resurgence of worry and anxiety? Is there anything you can do today to affect a positive outcome? If there is, have you taken the necessary action? If the answer is no, what do you need to do in order to "turn it over?"

Remember, whether you want to let go, or *need* to let go, the same formula applies: *You take your focus (obsessive or otherwise) off of the relationship or circumstance that you wish to leave, and put that same energy into walking towards your own light.*

In other words, look in the opposite direction, keep your attention on what energizes and enlivens you, and take steps towards it. When your head starts to swivel, ask yourself questions like:

- "If I weren't so fixated on this (what I'm leaving), what would I be thinking about?" or
- "What would it feel like if I could actually surrender and leave this behind?"

If your immediate reaction is, "What do you mean, what would I be thinking about? How can I possibly know in which direction to head? I'm still trying to figure out who I am and what I want," you need not worry. You have embarked upon a three-book series with that end in mind— to recover yourself, your passion, your purpose, and your joy. You are on the right path and have made a great beginning. So trust the process. It will only get better.

Reader Commitment to Letting Go

In order to free up some mental and emotional
energy, I commit to letting go of the following:

_____

_____

_____

Today's date: _____

Notes on Part Two

Part Three:
Establish and Maintain Boundaries

When all is said and done, there is probably nothing that contributes more to our busy, out-of-balance lifestyles than boundary issues. We don't know what appropriate boundaries look like, we don't know how to set limits, we don't honor our own boundaries, and we often step on the toes of others by not respecting theirs.

Boundary difficulties manifest in many ways. Our need to be liked, to do the right thing, and to please others can cause us to sacrifice to such a degree that we jeopardize our own balance in the process. Driven by the "shoulds," we say "yes" even when we know it will put us over the edge. Instead of being honest with what we can and cannot do, want or don't want, we just suck it up and do it anyway, thinking that this is our duty, the role we were meant to play.

Often we allow other people's opinions of us to become more important than our own. And so we conform and compromise, because we don't want to disappoint or to be in anyone's disfavor. Rather than speak up and have a voice, we are easily taken advantage of, controlled, manipulated, and dictated to. In the process, we can lose our integrity and, in some cases, ourselves.

On the flip side of the same boundary issue, we can have some very strong opinions regarding what *other* people are doing or not doing. We think *we* know what's best and we're not afraid to tell them. We think that we are the "expert" and so add our two cents worth and give suggestions, even when our opinion has not been sought. We don't see this as butting into what is "none of our business." Instead, we con ourselves into thinking we are just being helpful.

Even when we don't tell others to their face what we think, we can still spend an inordinate amount of time and energy talking about what they are doing, not doing, thinking about doing, once did, and so forth. We can literally spend hours caught up in lengthy diatribes about other people's lives which are, also, none of our business!

Our lack of boundaries can hit both extremes on the same spectrum. Simply put, we lack boundaries when:

- We consider it our job to make others happy.
- We make other people's opinions so important that we sacrifice our own integrity.
- We think what they are doing or not doing is our business, when in reality, it isn't.
- We frequently give suggestions even when they are not asked for, always with the conviction that we know best.
- We give time, money, or other resources which we really cannot afford to be giving.
- We say "yes" even though it will jeopardize our own schedules, balance, and/or budgets.
- We care for or try to please others at the expense of our own well being.

Make no mistake here. None of this is about being selfish or self-centered. It is about checking our underlying motives to determine if we are giving from a sincere desire to be helpful, or from a sense of shame, guilt, "should," the need for approval, or the need to be in charge. When motivated from any of the latter, we tend to run into problems. We frequently end up feeling used, resentful, over-extended, and under-appreciated.

Establishing and maintaining boundaries is, without a doubt, some of the most important work we can ever do if we want to free up energy, lighten our spirits, skip rather than trudge through our days, and finally—to enjoy that guilt-free downtime. So let's get going on this worthwhile endeavor!

How do we know if we've
done enough or given enough?
When we get to the point
where to do or give one more
little bit would cause us to
feel resentful or
taken advantage of.

Chapter Nine: Clarify Boundaries

Before we go any further, and because many of us are confused where boundaries are concerned, let's get some clarity regarding what they are all about. Boundaries are limits, rules, and guidelines that inform our own personal behavior and how we use our time and energy. They also determine what we consider appropriate behavior from others and how we respond when somebody steps outside of those parameters. Boundaries allow us to honor our own limits by not accepting or overdoing anything that compromises our health and integrity, and by not letting others determine what those limits are.

Healthy boundaries also indicate an understanding that we are not responsible for how other people think, feel, or act. It is not our job to tell them what to do, to rescue them, to try and figure out what they need, to solve their problems, make them happy, pay their bills, or to somehow "fix" them. Healthy boundaries allow us to support, validate, and help others to help themselves, without our taking personal ownership of their process or the outcome. We respect their rights to make their own decisions and choices, even when they are different from what we would want.

Good boundaries promote good, healthy relationships—not only with our significant others, but also with children, parents, friends, extended family, co-workers, and so on.

However, when boundaries are not clear, consistent, or don't exist, our relationships suffer. They can be exhausting, frustrating, difficult more often than not, or all-consuming. They can involve an ongoing struggle, create an emotional flux between euphoria and despair, or cause chronic feelings of urgency, anxiety, or agitation.

When we don't have healthy boundaries, we can go against our own personal integrity in order to please somebody else, making our emotional well-being dependent upon their mood, reaction, or opinion. Or we can take the opposite extreme, by trying to force our rules, standards, and desires on them. In either case, we can be quick to point the finger when things don't go the way we would like.

The truth is, most of our relationship difficulties have more to do with who <u>we</u> are than with who somebody else is. Once again, we are who we are for reasons long past. And the ways in which we relate (or don't) to others, the boundaries we have (or don't have), our tendency to struggle (or not) within our relationships are most always related to the people, situations, and circumstances we encountered during early childhood.

In fact, most, if not all, professionals who work with human behavior agree that there is a direct correlation between early childhood experiences and current confusion/difficulty within relationships. This can be *especially true* for those raised in dysfunctional family systems, such as homes with alcoholism or other addictions, mental illness, rage-aholism, inconsistency, extreme chaos or abuse, or those who might have experienced early trauma or loss which was not dealt with adequately.

Pia Mellody, an author renowned and respected as a leading authority and educator for those who were raised in dysfunctional environments, coined the term "co-dependents." She said that for children who grew up in unstable, inconsistent, or abusive homes, maintaining personal boundaries can be especially problematic.

Melody Beattie, who wrote *Codependent No More,* went so far as to compile a list of the patterns and characteristics of the co-dependent or "adult child." These personality traits run the gamut from extreme compliance to extreme control, both of which are red flags for boundary issues.

Beattie believes that Adult Children of any dysfunction have some or all of the following traits which create problems within relationships. According to her, an Adult Child can:

- Compromise values to avoid rejection or anger from others.
- Become extremely loyal, even in harmful situations.
- Fail to ask others to meet needs.
- Value the opinion of others more than our own; be afraid to express differing opinions and feelings.
- Put aside own interests to do what others want.
- Freely offer advice and direction without being asked.
- Need to be needed in order to have relationships.
- Attempt to convince others how they "should" think, feel.
- Use sex for approval and acceptance.

If you identify with more than a couple of these characteristics, you will probably want to investigate further by reading books by either of these authors. In the meantime, there is really good news about all of this:

If our relationship problems and our boundary issues are related to our own attitudes, assumptions, perceptions, and behaviors (and most of them are), these are all things that we have the power to identify and change.

So where do we begin? How do we get from here to there? Well, for openers, let's look at what it is like to have good boundaries within a relationship.

Probably the biggest indicator of a relationship with healthy boundaries is that there is a fairly even distribution of give and take between the parties involved. Granted, there are circumstances in all of our lives when we might be more needy or giving than the other person, but healthy relationships can accommodate these.

When we have good boundaries, we are able to be clear and consistent about what is acceptable and what is not. We feel safe. We have a voice and can express how we feel about *anything* without being afraid of being judged. We can even disagree without fearing negative consequences such as criticism, anger, sarcasm, deadly silence, raised eyebrows, sulking, passive/aggressive behavior, yelling, slamming doors, threatening to leave, etc. We can even be wrong every now and then and expect to be forgiven. And, once again, this does not just pertain to relationships with significant others, but also includes those with friends, co-workers, adult children, extended family, and so forth.

Relationships are not intended
to be exhausting, constantly
frustrating, extremely difficult
or all-consuming.

When we have healthy boundaries, we respect that people want different things in life, do things in ways that differ from how we might do them, or have varying opinions and beliefs from ours. Instead of constantly trying to "drag them" into thinking, acting, and believing the same ways we do, we attempt to "meet others where they are." And we respect the fact that we deserve the same in return.

When our boundaries are clear and consistent, and our relationships feel safe, we are then able to work through differences and difficulties as they arise. Instead of sweeping things under the carpet, stuffing our feelings, exploding inappropriately, or taking on angst that is not ours to own, we learn to compromise and can come to actual resolutions. Rather than feel as if we are habitually walking on eggshells, we feel respected, validated, and valued. And when that is the reality, we have a much better chance of becoming all of who we might be. Don't we all deserve that?

Exercise 11: Relationship Inventory – Best or Stressed

Before going further, let's pause for a few moments to take a quick inventory of the current relationships in our lives.

Sit quietly and think about everybody with whom you are currently involved in one way or another. This includes anyone who requires your time, energy, or attention, even those individuals that you may not see often or at all, but who still consume your mental and emotional energy. Begin by just listing the principal players on the left side of the following chart. Don't forget your pets. And remember to be "curious, not critical."

Relationships Time/Energy Awareness Chart

outgoing energy (-)	incoming energy (+)

After you compile this list, go through it again and think about which of these relationships feels reciprocal. This refers to those with whom you feel safe, supported, and able to be who you really are. People who give something back to the relationship. (Our pets are usually really good at this!) Make a checkmark on the right side of the chart for any of those who fall into this category.

For names that fail to get this checkmark, you may need to delve a little deeper. The first thing to consider is this: "Does this person drain my energy while giving nothing in return? If so, why do I maintain a relationship with them?"

Do you need to? If they are a family member, most likely the answer is yes. But even then, do you need to be in relationship with this person to the extent to which you are? Come on now, really?

There are other questions regarding those personalities who only get mentioned on the left side of the chart. These deserve some serious consideration:

- Are you the one always expected to go the extra mile, to reach out, make the phone call, or the plans? What do you think would happen if you stopped doing that? Would the relationship cease?

- Do you tend to make excuses for the other person when they fail to return calls, emails, or cancel plans at the last minute? Why?

- Does this relationship exhaust you because of your own expectations placed upon this person or this relationship? Are your expectations realistic or simply wishful thinking?

- What would happen if you just accepted this person exactly as they are right now? If you realized that you don't have to fix them or solve their problems? Would you feel a sense of relief? Would your energy be restored?

- Do any of these individuals exhaust you because you are trying to accept behavior which is clearly unacceptable? If you even suspect this might be true, spend some time writing about this. You might want to speak to a trusted friend as well.

- If your inventory has indicated *multiple* personalities that drain you, can you understand how this might have more to do with who <u>you</u> are than with who <u>they</u> are? Why do you perpetuate these relationships? Is it because you have difficulty saying no? Do you really think you are supposed to be all things to all people?

Sometimes an inventory such as this will reveal one or two total crazy-makers who do nothing but siphon our energy. These are people who love to live in the chaos, to bend our ears repeatedly about their trials and tribulations, yet seldom take the necessary action to get out of their personal "ruts" and/or promote their own well-being. If you have one or several of these in your life, take a few minutes to examine the following. Once again, really think about your answers.

- Do I give this person more mental or emotional energy than is necessary? Why? Do I *really* think it is my job to come up with their solutions, or to change/fix them in some way?
- Have I willingly put myself in the role of the "go-to" person? Has this become a drain on my time and energy? Why do I continue to do this? Do I even know?
- What would happen if I started setting some limits with these people? Would it make me feel guilty, as if I were doing something wrong? Am I afraid that they wouldn't like me anymore?

This inventory is certainly not intended to make us even more overwhelmed or exhausted than we already are, or to find fault with ourselves in any way. At this point, we are just gathering information to increase our awareness. The good news is, for every problem, there is a solution. So now that we may have become a little uncomfortable due to some of the aforementioned questions, let's take some steps to move into that solution. Over the next several pages, we will learn to put together a "boundary toolkit," full of directions and tools that we can bring out and use for practically all of our relationship concerns.

More relationship problems
are related to our own
attitudes, assumptions and
perceptions. This is good
news as these are things
which can be changed.

Chapter Ten: Build a "Boundary Toolkit"

We all need help with boundaries. For some of us, our boundaries are too weak; for others, too rigid. Sometimes we vacillate between the two, which can be even more problematic. In many cases, we just don't know what we don't know. When it comes to how we relate and respond to friends, family members, significant others, and even to our work, we can be confused about what is right and reasonable and what is not; about what we "should" take the initiative for, and what others need to be doing for themselves; about what is our business and what isn't; about what we want to do, and what we feel has been put upon us.

In many cases, our biggest struggle is determining when enough is enough. When have we done enough, said enough, or given enough? How do we know? The answer is a simple one:

We've done, said, and given enough when we get to the point where to do, say, or give one more little bit would cause us to feel resentful or taken advantage of.

That said, the next question becomes this: "How do we begin to set some healthy limits where we have had none before?"

This answer is simple as well, although not a quick fix by any means. We must learn new behaviors, and pick up some new tools, all of which need to be easy to use and to maintain. After all, we're busy and we don't have time to over-think these things. So let's not waste another moment to begin putting together our own boundary toolkit.

The tool of honesty

Honestly is vital when it comes to setting healthy and appropriate boundaries. In this regard, honesty means knowing our own personal limits and limitations and conveying this same information to appropriate parties. This process also begins with an action that we have used throughout this book: self-inquiry. We ask *ourselves* some very important questions and answer truthfully. Because, in reality, it is usually with ourselves that we are the most dishonest.

Dishonesty is present every time we agree to do something that we don't want to, we don't have time for, or that we know is going to push us over the edge, and/or have a negative effect on those closest to us. Whenever we go against our better judgment or instincts and say "yes" to something we know will overextend us or make our life crazy, we are not being truthful. And this is a boundary issue.

How do we turn this behavior around, especially for those of us who have spent a lifetime discounting our own truth? Well, we have to start at the beginning, at the very moment we are asked to do something, bring something, buy something, and so forth. Instead of rushing right into agreement, we must learn to PAUSE, to take a moment to follow the "yes" through to the end. We can question ourselves honestly by asking, "Do I really want to do this?" or "How will this impact my own schedule or that of my family's?" And if by saying yes, we will be thrown off balance or pushed into undesired chaos, we must be truthful enough to say so. As selfish as this may initially feel, in these instances, "no" is an absolutely appropriate response. "No, I can't do it." "No, I can't make it." "No, it won't work." "No, this is not a good time." We don't have to come up with great and elaborate excuses (my Aunt Jennie died, the kids are sick, I think I'm coming down with the flu), nor do we need to justify our response, or apologize. We only need to be truthful with ourselves first and then convey this same honesty to others.

Several of us will have real difficulty with this. We have operated so long under the mistaken perception that if somebody asks us to do something, or they expect us to give of our time, energy, and resources, then the moral "Christian" thing is to say "yes." This has caused many of us to take on more than we can handle on a regular basis. In fact, to some, even the *thought* of saying "no" can feel wrong or selfish.

Yet, if we were *honest* with ourselves, and reviewed our past history, we would undoubtedly see that saying yes against our own better judgment ultimately leaves us feeling resentful at others or bad about ourselves, neither of which feels very good. So we really must find different ways to respond when we are asked to do something that we just don't have the time, energy, or resources to do.

This is a boundary that we're going to have to gently ease into because, let's face it: Saying "no" does not come easily! So instead of starting right out at this place, we can buy ourselves some time by first saying something like, "Let me think about this and get back to you. I'm

Setting boundaries will
certainly not make us
the most popular
person on the block.

not sure right now." If their response is, "Well, I really need to know right now," then we can go right to the "Well, in that case, I guess I will have to say no."

In the cases where we are given time to respond, and we have promised to get back to them, then we must be true to our word. If we tend to have trouble in this regard, we can begin by calling them at a time we know they won't be at home, and leaving our regrets on their voicemail. However, as time goes by and we become more confident with knowing and speaking our truth, we can be honest and direct right from the beginning and either respond with "no," or call them back when we have a good chance of getting them in person. And even if every shred of our being feels guilty when we first start setting these limits, this is how we begin to create good, mature, and self-respecting boundaries.

Of course, there is a flip side to this, in that we must also respect the boundaries of others when they are unable to grant a request. If we are given "no" for an answer, we must accept that and not take it personally. Everything is not all about us! We need to appreciate the fact that whatever we asked for just didn't work out for the other party at this time. It doesn't matter if we wanted them to have coffee, come to dinner, pick the kids up, give a jewelry party, fill in for us at work, or something else. If "no" is their answer, there is no need for us to question, manipulate, badger, or try to guilt them into changing their mind. We also don't have to get our feelings overly-hurt. We just need to accept that it is not going to work the way in which we had hoped. Oh, well... how important is it? And even when it seems important, we must act like a grownup and just get over it.

Once we start setting boundaries, we need to understand that we will **not** be the most popular person on the block. When we stop trying to please all the people all the time, people aren't pleased! But the healthy side of this is that they will eventually come to trust what we say as being the truth. And we know ourselves how nice it is when we don't have to second-guess somebody's responses or their motives, but can believe that they are saying what they mean. It's way past time we became one of those people! It makes it so much easier for all concerned.

Becoming honest with ourselves and with others is definitely a learning process that will take time, commitment, and practice. So when we are asked to do something, we must not be afraid to honestly ask ourselves (before responding, not after): "Do I really want to do this? Will it fit into my schedule/agenda?"

If our answers are "no" and we say "yes" anyway, we might ask ourselves another question, probably the biggest one where honesty is concerned: "What is my underlying motive here? Why am I saying "yes" when I really want to say "no"? And then we need to really pay attention to our answers so that we can learn something about ourselves. At least, that's the hope.

The tool of validation

Another boundary difficulty that we have is our tendency to put more time and emotional energy into people and situations than what is warranted. For instance, somebody calls us up or comes to us with a problem or concern and our immediate response is to feel somehow that it is our job to fix or solve their problem. This can be especially true when dealing with those high maintenance friends and family members who always seem to have some crisis going on, and who tend to bring their issues to *us*, often at the worst possible moment! Mistakenly believing that it's our job to "fix" them, we jump right into action. After all, we're the go-to person, he/she who can fix everything! Maybe we like the feeling of importance and power that this momentarily provides. But the price we pay is higher than we might think. This boundary issue is exhausting us!

Most people really don't want to be "fixed." What they want is to be heard and understood. And when we are so busy trying to figure out their solutions for them, we are not really listening to what they are saying! It's time we took a different approach. Instead of trying to solve, and/or resolve somebody else's crisis, we must learn to listen and *validate their feelings* instead. And it won't be as difficult as we might originally have thought. In fact, it will be a whole lot easier than what we've been doing!

The way this works is similar to playing a game of mental volleyball. The phone rings or the person shows up and they immediately start in with their litany of woes; in other words, they hit their emotional ball over to our side of the court and it is loaded with "issues." Now we have a choice. Do we take on these as though they were ours to own? Do we try to figure everything out and solve the other person's problems? *No, we don't.* Instead of assuming responsibility for something that does not belong to us, we simply tap the ball back onto their side of the court. And we do this by *validating their feelings*. "I hear you. That must feel really bad or scary or hurtful." This is where we begin.

Chances are that the ball will come flying back quickly with some more of the same. Once again, rather than grab hold of it, thinking it is ours to take care of, we gently tap it back again, this time saying something like, "Wow, sounds like you are having a really bad day." *More validation.*

When the other person pushes the ball back onto our side of the court (because let's be honest, some people are addicted to talking about the problem), we tap it back again, this time with a question that not only gives them full ownership of their own situation, but also encourages them to move out of the problem and into the solution. "Can you think of anything you can do about this?"

Most times, the ball will come back, especially if the other party would rather eat up our time and energy than take action on their own behalf. We know who these people are! Some might belong to that category we deemed "crazy-makers." Still, regardless of what they might want, we tap the ball back into their court once more. This time, we can do it by sharing how we might have reacted in a similar situation. For instance, "I remember a time when something like this happened to me, and the way I handled it was to...." We are still not telling them what to do or taking responsibility for figuring out what they need to do. The volleyball format keeps the conversation time-limited and honors their boundaries as well as our own.

So whether we are dealing with a co-worker, a family member, neighbor, or friend:

- We validate that we have heard them.
- We validate their feelings.
- We ask them what they could do to improve their own situation.
- We share how we have dealt with something similar.

Our time is not a commodity we can afford to throw away, and it is not our responsibility/job to fix anyone else. Even when our intentions are the best in the world, trying to fix is still controlling, condescending, or both. It drains our energy and it takes responsibility and dignity away from the other party by implying that they are not capable of handling their own issues.

We don't need to do this. We just need to be kind, to let the other person know that we hear them, to validate their feelings, thoughts, and tough times, to ask the appropriate questions, and to share our own experiences when relevant. And that is more than good enough. It is the beginning of healthy boundaries.

The tool of timing

Few would disagree that we live in an intrusive world. Whether at work, home, or even on vacation, people have become accustomed to showing up or calling with little or no consideration regarding whether or not it may be a good time for the other person. Think about it. How many

It is not our
responsibility to
fix anybody.

of us are sitting around twiddling our thumbs, waiting for the phone to ring? Yet, people behave as though we are! And we do the same. We call people at home without ever thinking that we may have caught them right in the middle of making dinner, helping the kids with homework, watching their favorite television program, paying bills, and so forth. Or we call our friends or significant others at work, without a thought as to whether or not they are in a position to speak to us.

When it comes to having good boundaries, the appropriate way to approach anybody, whether by phone or in person, is by beginning the conversation with the question, "Is this a good time?" This is a question born out of respect for the other person's agenda. Not only is it good manners, but by asking somebody whether or not it is a good time, we also give them the opportunity and permission to respond honestly when it is not. "Actually, I was headed out the door." Or, "I'm right in the middle of dinner." Then we can make arrangements to speak at another time.

This works both ways. We not only use timing to respect somebody else's boundaries, but also to protect ours. So when *we* get a phone call and *we* are in the middle of something, our appropriate (and honest) response is, "It's good to hear from you but I just sat down to help my child with homework. When would be a good time to call you back?" Or, even more outrageous, we could just not answer the phone when we're in the middle of something important!

The same is true within our physical spaces. Whether at home or in the office, it is not a good practice to just barge unannounced into a room, thinking the other party is sitting there waiting for us to arrive! Generally, people are in the middle of things. So, once again, we begin by saying—"Is this a good time?" Or when we see that it obviously isn't, to quickly excuse ourselves saying, "When you get a minute, let me know." It's all about respecting somebody else's time and space.

Timing is also essential for many of our face-to-face conversations, especially those of an intimate, difficult, or confrontational nature. In other words, it never works well to confront our spouse or child or friend with something we need to talk about the minute they walk through the door. It also doesn't work well to try and have a meaningful conversation when they are clearly involved or distracted with something else, or when they are obviously over-extended, in a bad mood, hungry, or tired. We don't interrupt a colleague in the middle of what appears to be an important task, or insist on being heard when others are not in a position to hear us. Choosing the wrong times for important conversations never gives us the results, or the relief, that we want or hope for.

If something is nagging us or bothering us, or we feel a need to talk about an issue, as much as we might want to get instant relief by sharing immediately with the concerned party, the more appropriate response is to make an appointment with the other person(s) to discuss the situation.

"There is something I want to talk with you about. Is this a good time? And, if it isn't, when would we be able to speak?"

Notice the language: A good time to talk *with* you, not *to* you. Nobody wants to be talked *to,* except maybe babies who don't have their voice yet. Talking *"to"* is condescending and very one-sided. Talking *with*, on the other hand, supposes much more equality. It is obvious which one opens the door to healthy communication!

The same holds true for protecting our own boundaries. When we are approached at the "wrong time" to have a conversation that we are not prepared to have in the moment, it is our responsibility to say, "I really do want to talk about this, but now is just not the time to do so." If the other person persists, we needn't get angry or defensive, just repeat our original statement, but perhaps give a time when we might be available. "This is not a good time but how about if we talk after dinner, or when the kids go to bed, or tomorrow when I've had a better night's sleep, or when I get a little more distance from whatever is going on."

We have a right to wait until the timing is better to discuss any emotional issue; and so do they. And we both have a right to make an appointment to do so. The importance of this boundary cannot be overstated. By making an appointment, we get that initial relief we're looking for, knowing that the "issue" will be discussed. And when we stop forcing conversations at times which are guaranteed to bring about disastrous results, we increase our chances of having a healthier, perhaps longer, and definitely more meaningful relationship. Timing really is everything.

The tool of clarity

Clarity is about "saying what we mean, meaning what we say, and not saying it meanly." It differs from, yet requires the honesty we spoke of earlier. And, it often involves our last tool of making an appointment to speak with somebody, especially regarding matters of an emotional nature.

As previously acknowledged, many of us have difficulty speaking the truth, and, in some cases, even knowing it.

We only know that something is bothering us; that something doesn't feel right. And even when we think we do know what the issues are, we can still struggle with being clear in our communication with the appropriate parties. Once again, we need some directions, some help learning to convey what we want and need to say without confusion, drama, or distraction.

The following format is going to help us with this. It gives us a basis upon which to clarify our own feelings, wants, and needs, and then to go one step further by sharing this information in a clear and honest manner with the parties involved. It is similar to, but a bit more comprehensive than, a format used in a previous section of this book. In this case, redundancy is a good thing.

Our new format goes like this: "I feel…, when you…, I need…"

I feel…. "disrespected, wounded, confused, like a little kid, unsafe, dismissed, invalidated, less than, unimportant, invisible, hurt, scared, angry, abandoned, rejected, like you're mad at me, taken advantage of, like a doormat, as if I've done something wrong…"

When you.... "tell me what to do and how to do it, interrupt me, roll your eyes while I'm speaking, yell, are late, treat me with sarcasm, don't respond, hide behind your paper, ignore me, fail to return my emails or phone calls, clam up, micromanage me, don't pull your fair weight, talk back..."

I need you to... "pay attention, speak in a civilized tone, answer me, show up on time, put the paper down, start taking responsibility, respond to me when I ask you something, stop interrupting, get back to me in a timely fashion, listen to me, stop telling me what to do, step up to the plate..."

This is a great format, especially helpful for us to begin *identifying* our own boundaries. Prior to now, we may never have even asked ourselves how we feel about a given situation and what we would like to see changed. Or we may have felt powerless over being able to communicate our feelings with confidence and clarity. In these cases, it would probably be helpful to begin by writing the format out and filling in the blanks. This can be a very beneficial exercise as it helps us really become clear about what the issues are, how we genuinely feel about what is happening or not happening, and about what might make things better; in other words, what would be a good outcome for all involved?

Writing not only increases our awareness, but it also gives us an opportunity to double check our own "stuff." We want to make sure we are not contributing to the problem in any way; for instance, by demanding more attention than is right or reasonable, being verbally abusive ourselves, trying to control the other person, not carrying our own weight, making demands instead of requests, giving mixed messages, and so forth. Being willing to examine our own part in any situation is a sure sign of emotional growth and maturity.

After we write things down and our clarity increases, we can then go on to share how we feel with others. Definitely a new approach for those of us prone to feeling powerless, sitting and stewing, sucking it up, stuffing it down, giving the silent treatment, internalizing our feelings, or yelling to "get our point across." In fact, in the beginning, speaking our truth may feel awkward, even out and out wrong. This is especially true if we are not used to asking for what we want and need, or if we are prone to accepting inappropriate behavior. In these cases, we may have to work especially hard to stay focused when sharing so that those to whom we are speaking do not distract us with their responses. Many are masters at getting us off course, so we need to keep it really simple, and continue coming back to our format, "I feel, when you, I need..."

As difficult as this can be, we must remember that *we teach others how to relate to us.* And even when the significant players are not keen on our requests or quick to respond or honor them, we speak them anyway. We don't say one thing one minute and something else the next, but remain clear, focused, and consistent. (Much easier if we've written ourselves a "cheat sheet.")

Before speaking, it is also important to know our bottom line; in other words, what are the consequences if the same behavior continues. We don't need to share this initially as we want to give others the opportunity to respond in the ways we would prefer. However, if over a period of time

Being willing to examine
our own part in any
situation is a sure sign of
emotional growth
and maturity.

the outcome is not what we want/need, we can add an additional step by expanding our format:

"I feel..., when you..., I need..., I am prepared to..."

I am prepared to..."stop reaching out to you, take such and such away (especially if dealing with kids/adolescents), leave the conversation if you continue raising your voice, stop being the one to always make the plans, let you pay the consequences of your behavior..."

And of course, the ultimate bottom line: "I am prepared to leave this relationship, job, career, or situation."

Sometimes, this is our only choice, especially in cases where we are being harmed in any way. And although there are different degrees of what might be considered harmful—from outward or passive hostility, to being treated "less than," talked down to, ignored, or on the receiving end of constant criticism or sarcasm—it is our personal responsibility to set boundaries that not only keep us safe, but also prevent us from compromising our basic integrity. As painful as leaving a relationship or situation can be, if we are being treated like a doormat, we are the only ones who can pick ourselves up off the floor.

Chapter Eleven: Stop Controlling!

Like many of our other behaviors, our need to control had its origin a long time ago. In the past, it may well have been our misguided attempts to feel safe and secure. If for any reason we grew up with a life that mimicked a game of musical chairs—when we didn't know what was going to happen next or when—it is to be expected that we would invest a lot of energy being in charge of the music, knowing where all the players are, and keeping track of the number of chairs. If we grew up with little or no self-worth, we may have learned to deflect attention from ourselves by focusing on what we think everybody else needs, even to the point of jumping in and directing their lives rather than allowing them to learn by their own mistakes and successes.

Needing to control is a direct violation of the boundaries of others. And as much as we may want to deny it, many of us would have to admit that we have had our moments of trying to control others, manipulate situations, and force outcomes. Dress these behaviors up as we might, our attempts to direct, micromanage, or dominate is at the bottom of many of our relationship difficulties.

We know we're controlling when we make ourselves the "director," telling others when to jump and how high. This is the control that convinces us we are responsible to solve every problem, not just our own, but everyone else's as well. Manipulation also plays a role in this because, after all, we know what's best and we have some well-honed methods of influencing the results we want.

There are obvious and not-so-obvious signs of a controlling nature. And let us be clear about one thing: Not only do these have their origin in the past, but they are also rooted in fear. That's right—fear. We fear that things won't get done, or won't get done *right,* unless we take charge of them. We fear that if we don't do/overdo for others, even when we haven't been asked, they won't like us or they won't be able to manage. We fear that if we don't take over, nobody else will. We are afraid that if things go wrong, we will somehow be blamed. We fear we will be judged because of what somebody else is doing or not doing and so we tell others exactly what to do and exactly how to do it—often.

Some of the obvious symptoms of control as an issue include:

- We have a need for things to be perfect.
- We have a habit of telling others what to do.
- Achieving the desired outcome is of utmost importance.
- We frequently check up on people to make sure they are doing things right (micromanaging).
- We force our opinions into situations that are really none of our business.
- We do more than what is right and reasonable for others, hindering their own growth and development in the process.
- We try to "push the river" in the direction we want it to go, regardless of the mental, emotional, and physical cost to us or others.

Those are the obvious signs of being controlling. But there are others which, while more subtle, are still symptomatic.

- We seldom speak our own truth.
- We are not honest about our own needs/wants.
- We say we're okay and it's fine when we aren't and it isn't.

We might not think of these things as controlling but let's look a little closer. Why do we not speak our own truth or share what we want or need? What are our underlying motives for not being honest? Why do we insist everything is okay when, in reality, it isn't? Could we be trying to control a situation by not creating any waves?

Control is one of those many illusions under which we've become accustomed to living. Rather than actually being in control, the greater reality is that whatever or whomever we're trying to exert power over is controlling us; rather than empowered, our insistence on being in the driver's seat keeps us preoccupied; our fixation on others often causes our own life to feel unmanageable; it doesn't make us all that popular with those around us; and it keeps us light years away from our own dreams and goals. Clearly, it isn't working.

So how do we change this dynamic? What steps can we possibly take to stop micromanaging, controlling, and/or manipulating? Well, we can begin by adding a few more tools to our "toolkit in process"; ones appropriately called:

- Self-care
- Restraint
- Proper perspective

Authentic self-esteem
can only be achieved
by doing esteem-able acts.

The tool of self-care

Balance and self-care are the number one tools to counteract our needs to be in charge of everything and everyone. When we take good care of ourselves, we are seldom as concerned about what others are doing or not doing. It really is that simple. When our own priorities are in place, we are much more apt to accept and respect the fact that everyone else has his/her own journey as well. When we are calm and centered, we have much less need to manipulate, take charge of, butt in, or try to steer others in the direction we think they should be going. In other words, we are able to "mind our own business"!

At the same time, when we are in balance, we are not so easily guilt-ed or manipulated into accommodating somebody else's needs or agenda at the expense of our own well-being.

It is also true, however, that the minute we put our own needs on the back burner, and become over-extended, overwhelmed, and/or totally off balance, our control issues come quickly screaming to the forefront. All of a sudden, nobody is doing anything right, fast enough, or to our satisfaction. Everything is wrong. We know this is true; that our tendency to micromanage and find fault is much more prevalent when we are not doing for ourselves what we need to be doing, as is our susceptibility to being controlled by others.

When we find ourselves back in control mode or see that we are resorting to our people-pleasing behavior, our first line of defense is to stop, turn around, and bring our attention and energy back to ourselves.

The question we ask ourselves is, "How well am I taking care of myself these days?" And if we've forgotten or neglected to utilize some of our healthy self-care tools, we might want to go back to the beginning of this book and review some of them before we get into further difficulties.

Remember, when we take care of ourselves, everyone ultimately benefits. And when we don't, we all pay a price.

The tool of restraint

Without a doubt, it can be confusing to determine what is simply being helpful and what is controlling. Overall, a good rule of thumb is to notice the frequency with which we make the same suggestions. If we have a habit of making the same suggestions with great regularity, this is a sure sign that we are attempting to control others and outcomes that are, in reality, far beyond our control. Not only do we create resistance and annoyance from those involved, but we also miss essential moments in our own lives because of this.

It's time we practiced a little self-restraint. Just because we think we know what's best, doesn't necessarily mean that it's true. And we certainly don't need to convey that information to the other party by insisting they do things our way and in our time. Just because we want everything perfect and looking good does not give us the right to dictate and direct those around us into doing what is necessary to bring about *our* desired results. Just because something is bothering us in the

When we take care
of ourselves,
everyone ultimately benefits.
And when we don't,
we pay a price.

moment does not give us license to discuss it at a time that is obviously not good for somebody else. Self-restraint is our answer.

It might be helpful to remind ourselves once again that control is all about fear; fear that we won't get what we want or need, fear that we will lose what we have, or fear that things won't work out the ways in which we would prefer. This does not go unnoticed.

We need to stop. When tempted to give unsolicited advice as though we were the expert on somebody else's life, or insist they do it our way and in our time, we can learn to practice restraint instead. This is about learning to control ourselves. We refrain from jumping in, raising our voice to make a point, adding our two cents, or giving unsolicited advice, no matter how much we want to!

Understandably, restraint isn't something that will come easily to many of us. The following exercise will give us some tools.

Exercise 12: Practice Restraint

When we attempt to control or manipulate others, situations, or outcomes, we exert time and energy that would be better spent elsewhere. So when we feel the need to do this, let's instead stop the momentum by taking a minute to ask ourselves some pertinent questions:

Giving suggestions
with great regularity
and repeating them
often is a sure
sign of trying to control
others and outcomes etc.

- Do I need to say this? Do I need to say it now? Do I need to say it in this tone of voice?

- Would I be better off to W.A.I.T. by questioning: Why am I talking?

- Do I realize that by telling others what to do, when to do it and how to do it, I am robbing them of the opportunity to learn, to grow, to profit by their own mistakes, and to evolve? Is this really fair?

- Am I focused on this situation or person because my own self-care is not what it should be right now? What do I need to do to take better care of myself in the moment?

- What would happen if I suddenly stopped being the director or dictator of somebody else's life? What is the underlying fear? Is this something I could or should write about?

- If I am feeling a sense of urgency to interfere or take control of somebody or something that really is none of my business, can I make a decision to wait a day or so before picking up the phone, pushing the "send" button, or verbalizing my opinions? Could I instead call a friend to discuss my concerns and feelings?

- What would it take for me to try these new behaviors for a week?

The tool of proper perspective

The last instrument in our boundary tool kit involves becoming right-sized; putting ourselves into proper perspective; knowing that we are not the end all and the be all; we are not the boss, the dictator, the director. We'll examine this concept in greater detail in the next and final section of this book, *Connect with the Real*. But before we move on, let's take a moment to really think about and fill in our Reader Commitment on boundaries.

<u>Reader Commitment to Healthier Boundaries</u>

In order to establish and maintain healthy
boundaries, I commit to doing the following:

_____

_____

_____

Today's date: _____

Notes on Part Three

Part Four:
Connect with the *Real*

We are moving along in our quest to create more physical and emotional balance, while establishing and maintaining better boundaries. This is a great thing. If we have put some of the suggestions offered into action, we have undoubtedly reaped the benefits of doing so. But we definitely aren't finished yet, as there is another vital component to balance that we have not addressed—that of the spiritual. And even though we have waited until the end of this book to discuss it, spiritual awareness and growth are as essential to authentic living as practically nothing else.

It cannot be argued that, in our overly-busy lifestyles, many of us have lost connection with our own true Self and lost sight of our ultimate purpose. We long to feel connected and fulfilled, yet are confused about how to proceed. We know something is missing, but we are not even sure what it is! So we struggle and claw and clamor and claim, only, in many ways, to reinforce and maintain our discontent, driven-ness, and emptiness.

There are many signposts that we have spiritual needs that are not being met:

- We feel disconnected, fragmented, and inwardly alone.
- We develop habits and behaviors which satisfy our longing in the short term, but ultimately create an even greater sense of emptiness.
- We expend a lot of time, energy, and focus on keeping up appearances.
- We can quickly fall into fear, negative thinking, or sadness.

- We become easily overwhelmed and can feel stuck or immobilized, OR
- We feel compelled to keep busy at all times, at any cost.
- Our intuition feels stymied and we're not sure what to do next or how and when to do it.
- We live with an underlying sense of missing *something,* feeling light years away from the life that wants to live in us.

Together, these symptoms could be classified as "cosmic unrest." But call them what we might, they are all signs that spiritual recovery is necessary. This is the work we are called upon to do next. It is the way we will reconnect, or in some cases, connect for the first time, with what we've been looking for all along—the *Real.*

Chapter Twelve: Understand "Cosmic Unrest"

Why is it that so many of us are resistant when it comes to the topic of spirituality? And why are we so quick to overlook or to discount our own spiritual needs? There are reasons, of course. For openers, we have become so accustomed to *more* and *now*—to obtaining immediate relief and measurable results—that the thought of acknowledging needs that don't have a quick fix is foreign to us. Our resistance might also be tied in with a mistaken assumption that spirituality is somehow connected to religion of one kind or another, a topic that for many can be loaded with emotional triggers. This is especially true if we were raised in strict religious environments which did the opposite of what they intended, resulting in our feeling judged, shamed, or wronged.

We can also be closed to the idea of spirituality if we grew up in homes where any mention of such was looked upon with ridicule, disdain, or from a vantage point of intellectual superiority; or in environments where the subject was never mentioned at all. In either case, is it any wonder that we, too, adopted the same mindsets and attitudes? And how about those of us who grew up just trying to survive? With all of our energy necessarily focused on doing what needed to be done in challenging circumstances, why would we have even thought about spirituality as a way of gaining insight, energy, wisdom, or even relief?

Even those of us who aren't closed to the idea, and in fact, may consider ourselves as already spiritual, religious, or both, might want to look a little deeper. How well do our beliefs translate into our everyday life? Do we feel calm, centered, whole, and complete? Or are we still far removed from our authentic selves and the Real?

Whatever our personal orientation is or is not, the consequences can be the same. Our spirits have become dampened and dormant, and our cosmic unrest has grown to such proportions that it drives and drains us. Let's look at how this might have come about.

When we were born, we came complete with a small spark of the Divine within; spiritual wisdom, intuition, and energy. For anybody who has experienced the birth of a child, or who has looked into the eyes of any infant, this spark is highly evident. Not only are a newborn's eyes full of peace, but they also reveal a great and deep "knowing."

This inner light could be likened to an internal compass, our own personal GPS system which is uniquely qualified to guide us on our journey; an energy source which contains the answers to those questions we so often ponder: "Who am I?" and "Where do I belong?"

Yet, even though we are born with this essential knowledge, from the moment of our birth it begins to get displaced, buried beneath a host of life occurrences. People placed in our path, circumstances we encounter, and distractions we get caught up in, all contribute to a "disconnect." In most cases, before we even have the opportunity to develop an intimate relationship with our intuitive "Self," this Divine spark becomes smothered beneath a pile of emotional rubble. As this innate knowledge of ourselves gets buried and lost, so does our connection to that which is

Eternal. Simultaneously, our cosmic unrest is born. In many ways, it also becomes our driving force. But we don't know this, so we end up making choices and taking actions which merely exacerbate rather than satisfy our inner longing for what's *Real*.

We become unduly attached to how things look. We develop and maintain habits and behaviors which ultimately backfire and sabotage. We expend tons of time and energy trying to manipulate, control, or change others. We get caught up in the familiar traps of acquisition and achievement. We become addicted to all matter of things and distract ourselves in ways too numerous to mention. We overuse alcohol, drugs, food, and technology. We sleep too much, watch mindless television for hours on end, and/or cram our calendars with commitments and activities that keep us busy but not fulfilled. And as the years pass, instead of being confident and joy-filled, we become further and further removed from what is real and true, and more and more driven by what is not.

Depending upon personal circumstances, we pick up additional emotional baggage that further prevents us from accessing this Divine inner spark: guilt, shame, self-reproach, remorse, unhealed pain, low self-esteem, secrets of which we become the keeper, and, of course, fear in a thousand guises. We addressed several of these in a previous section of this book. This separation becomes more pronounced and problematic over time, as we learn to be tuned out instead of tuned in.

This is <u>not our fault</u> or anyone else's. We are who we are for reasons, and most of these reasons are reasons long past. It just is what it is. The following exercise and illustration will demonstrate this concept even further.

Exercise 13: Identify Barriers to Self/Higher Energy

The center of the following circle represents your Divine Spark of Self at birth. The outer circles indicate feelings and behaviors which you have picked up over time and placed between you and this inner Self. It is important to understand that most of this was done on an unconscious level. And while each wall was initially erected for reasons, in many cases these reasons no longer exist. Yet, we continue to maintain these barriers without really being aware of it. This keeps our inner spirit under wraps, our intuition and wisdom stifled and inaccessible, and leaves us feeling little or no connection to the Real.

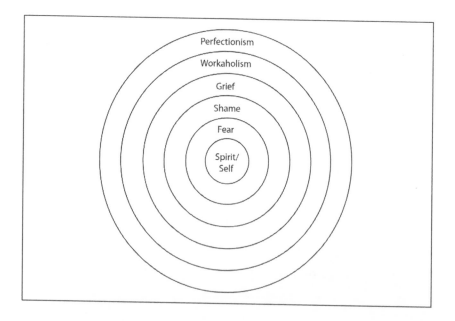

This is a simplified example of what the process of separation looks like. There is, of course, far more to this concept, which will be addressed in this book's sequel. However, this is a good place to start. So take a moment to think about and write down any "walls" you may knowingly or unconsciously have erected throughout the years. This is anything that keeps you separated from your own true self. You probably identified several in the previous sections of this book.

As you do this exercise remember, as always, to be "curious not critical." After all, we are only recovering some necessary information in order to increase our awareness. This is where change begins.

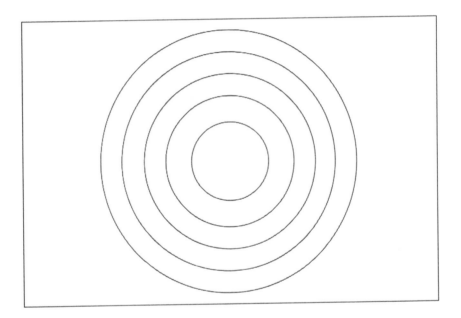

Chapter Thirteen: Begin Spiritual Recovery

We live in two worlds simultaneously: the outer world in which we take care of the daily business of living; and the inner world, which contains the core of who we really are—the Self which is Eternal and which is connected to The Eternal. However, the problem is, we are so accustomed to functioning as human doings rather than human beings, we tend to place most of our attention and energy on the people, places, and outer circumstances of our lives. In the process, we inadvertently neglect our inner reality and spiritual needs, failing to realize that we come with an expiration date.

Due to the phenomenon of Grace, we are periodically woken up by moments of clarity in which we are reminded that there is so much more than meets the eye. We may not call these by name, but we have all had times of being briefly distracted from our external and internal busy-ness, and given an opportunity to connect with our authentic Selves; little spiritual interruptions during which we know beyond a doubt that we are part and parcel of a much larger reality.

These spiritual experiences, or moments of truth, might be as extraordinary as witnessing the birth of a child, or as insignificant as catching a glimpse of sunlight bouncing off a lake. We might feel connected with something "Eternal" while standing under the brilliance of the full moon, looking deeply into the eyes of our beloved, sitting on top of a mountain, or watching a spectacular sunset. Unplanned and unanticipated, these little interruptions to our normal way of functioning can bring momentary feelings of deep peace and satisfaction. We are not only afforded a glimpse of our Eternal Self, but also feel spiritually connected to something Greater; something beautiful, something real, something permanent and unending. For just a second, we know deep within that all is right where it is supposed to be, including us. Our challenge is to make these moments more the norm than the exception.

But, of course, we have trouble doing this. First off, most of us are so darn busy, the moment we have one of these glimpses, rather than linger with the feeling, we quickly move into "doing." And secondly, when it comes to the concept of "eternal" or "spiritual," many of us carry preconceived prejudices and personal orientations which keep us closed off from, or resistant to, exploring further. As mentioned previously, this is especially true for those who liken these words to religion, and whose past experiences may not have been positive.

Let's stop for a moment to see if we belong to this group. The following inventory should tell us a lot.

Exercise 14: Take a Spiritual Inventory

Check any of the following with which you identify:

_____ I was raised in a religious environment with a "God" who was punishing, demanding, and rule-oriented. Concepts such as "Eternal" or "Higher Power" just seem like more of the same from my perspective.

We may not know them
as such, but most of us
have had authentic
spiritual experiences.

____ I have tried the way of "faith" in the past, but it just hasn't worked well for me.

____ Things of a spiritual nature were never discussed in my family of origin. And if they were, it was done disparagingly or with a hint of intellectual superiority.

____ I'm not sure why, but I have always had resistance when it comes to anything of a spiritual or religious nature. After all, just look at the world!

____ In my home of origin, we were told one thing in the name of religion, yet we were shown the exact opposite.

For those who already consider themselves "enlightened" or "spiritual," it might be beneficial to look a little closer:

- How well does spirituality impact my everyday life? Does it have a positive influence on how I think, act, and feel?
- Do I use spiritual resources to alleviate or mediate such things as fear, self-doubt, insecurity, anger, and resentment? Does this help me feel grounded and secure?
- When situations arise which baffle and confuse me, do I quiet myself down, go within, or meditate to find the answers? Do I feel intuitive and guided, or do I tend to force solutions instead?
- Do I take active steps to connect with my inner Self and to that which is Eternal? Or do I think this is something that should just happen on its own?

- How well do my beliefs serve me or others? Do I wish for greater freedom from my thoughts and emotions? Do I habitually race hither and yon, not quite sure where I'm going? Or awake in the morning feeling overwhelmed, anxious, and inwardly isolated?
- And of course, there is the biggest question of all:

"Am I living the life that wants to live in me?"

It doesn't matter how disconnected, resistant, or full of cosmic unrest we might feel *right now;* we can still turn this dynamic around. And it doesn't matter what our past prejudices and preconceptions may or may not be; we can still get over and beyond them. Although this will be a stretch for some, all we really need to do is become open-minded and willing to take suggestions. If we can manage to do that, old messages and concepts will soon be replaced with something that works a whole lot better.

How exactly can we do this? How can we get from here to there? What actions do we need to take?

Well, we can begin by just making a decision; a decision to lay aside any previous thoughts, convictions, or prejudices regarding spirituality that might stand in the way of our taking some new suggestions. Once we make this decision, we can then come up with a new concept of spirituality, one that will work for us and with us. This will not be as difficult as we might imagine, as there are many practices, beliefs, and concepts which are very much at home under the wide umbrella which spirituality casts. If we look closer, we will probably realize that we are already familiar with many of them.

Exercise 15: Decide and Reconsider

Spirituality

Meditation   Tai Chi   Music   Prayer
        Gratitude   Ritual   Yoga   Art   Passion
Psalms   Reike   labyrinth
                 Chanting   Journaling   Creativity
Dance   Nature
                  Soul   Service   Love   play
Fellowship
        Literature   Humor   Sexuality   Gardening
Beauty

Stop for a moment to look at the words written under the umbrella. Do any of them jump right out at you? Are there any practices that you currently use to engage with your inner Self? Or, if there used to be, but you have put the practice on the back burner because your life became too busy, is it possible to reinstate it? Make a decision to begin.

If there is nothing to which you can currently relate or that interests you, can you come up with some other activity or suggestion that might help you recover some spiritual energy?

While you are thinking about this, also give some thought to the concept of a Higher Power or Higher Consciousness. What sort of image or idea does this conjure up for you? Is it related to a specific religious belief or a God of your understanding? If so, and it works for you, this is well and good. If not, or if this is a completely new consideration, come up with your own image of Higher Power/Spiritual Energy, one that aligns with your personal beliefs or non-beliefs. What characteristics and qualities would you give this Higher Energy? Perhaps you'd choose those of a kind friend, teacher, parent or grandparent, or mentor who always made you feel special, safe, protected, loved, and heard. Depending on your background, you might also consider the positive qualities of some religious or spiritual leader: Jesus or Mary or Buddha or Gandhi or the Holy Spirit or the Divine. Or maybe your Higher Power is more related to the idea of Higher Purpose or Grace or nature or weather or planets or angels. Remember: This is your own concept and can be whatever works the best for you. So stop whatever you are doing for a minute and really give this some serious thought. Write about it. This simple exercise could be the beginning of enormous change in your outer and inner life.

Where spiritual matters
are concerned, we have the
ability to clear the slate
and start anew
beginning right now.

Chapter Fourteen: Access the Inner World

Coming up with a new understanding of spirituality is only the first step towards connecting with our inner Self/Truth. There are several other suggestions we can utilize to connect and engage with the Divine life force within us as well as tap into a Higher Consciousness. We must remember that both are realities that already exist; we just need to find ways to access them. And the way we go about this process is by moving in two directions at the same time—from the inside-out and from the outside-in.

We move from the inside-out by taking active individual measures to awaken that Divine spark deep within us which has long been dormant. It might help to think about this as an internal candle that has nearly been snuffed out, but continues to hold the flame. Our job is to find ways to fan this flame and bring the fire back to life.

We move from the outside-in by enlisting the help of a Higher Energy Field. It makes no difference whatsoever what we believe or don't believe in this regard; only that we believe there is something greater than us!

When addressed from both directions at the same time, our chances of breaking through those barriers we have unconsciously erected over the years increase considerably. The process will look like this:

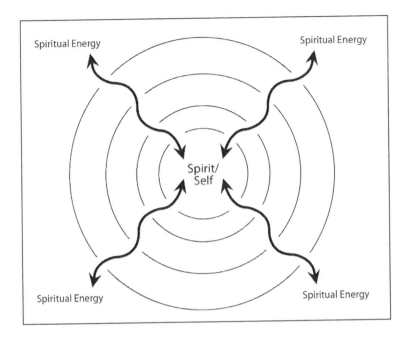

This process absolutely requires us to be active participants. So as you read through this next section of suggestions, think about *one* practice or action you can begin immediately. The rest can be added as you go along.

Listen to meaningful music

Turn off the television, put your iPhone away, and listen to some meaningful music instead. No matter who we are, there are few other things that can so thoroughly permeate our defenses, open up our hearts, and transport us beyond what is tangible. Music truly is the universal language of the soul. If we want to awaken our sleeping spirit, listening to music that resonates with us is a great and easy way to begin. Whether in our cars or in our homes, it is time to become intentional in our selection of music and pick stations and CDs which have songs that touch the core of our very being. If we don't know where to begin, we can go to a music store and ask for advice, or speak to some of our "spiritually-attuned" friends. This could be a fun thing to experiment with!

Develop the morning routine

If we want to become more intentional, insightful, and more spiritual, we must begin our day in ways that support these goals. *The way in which we begin our day will determine how well (or not) we will live it.*

To that end, a morning "spiritual" routine is absolutely essential. In a previous chapter, it was suggested that we take a few minutes each morning to reflect upon the upcoming day. We are now encouraged to go one step further by adding some additional practices during this morning period. These can include such things as intentional prayer, journaling, and/or some form of meditation; all of which will require additional time and space. That means we may need to get up fifteen or twenty minutes earlier each morning and also find a quiet place where we won't be disturbed by children, animals, spouses, or phone calls. We might even assign a certain area in our home for this morning routine, perhaps creating a special altar or table on which to place objects or pictures of special significance. This is all about setting the stage for quieting our minds and going within. Its importance cannot be underestimated.

Extend an invitation

In the very beginning, we can keep our morning routine simple. After all, this is not about adding more "busy-ness" or stress into our lives! Plus, the simpler we make it, the greater our chances for long term success, which is what we are looking for.

We could start by lighting a candle and inviting/invoking Spiritual Energy, or Higher Good, or God, or Holy Spirit, into our day and into our lives. Just a simple invitation is all it takes to begin breaking through our resistance and self-made barriers in order to open up to spiritual wisdom and insight. And, once again, it doesn't matter what we believe or don't believe. All we need to do is have the willingness to extend some kind of invitation to some Universal Energy/Higher Power to be with us on our daily journey. What do we possibly have to lose by giving this a try?

This invocation is the most pivotal and powerful prayer we will ever extend, because once we do, the energy will begin to shift. It doesn't even matter what we say or how we make our request; it is only important that we do. If we have difficulty with this, it might help to think about how we might speak to a close and trusted friend or loved one.

Read and relate

We can add another tool to our morning ritual by incorporating a small inspirational reading directly after our prayer of invitation. It doesn't take long and this will also help us to let go of old concepts (which don't work) and develop some new ones. There are many wonderful daily meditation books written expressly for this purpose: *The Daily Word* by Unity, *365 Days Around the World* by Emmet Fox, *Streams in the Desert* by L.B. Cowman, *The Language of Letting Go* or *Journey to the Heart* by Melody Beattie are but a few. Some men and women enjoy reading the Scriptures or poetry, such as that written by Rumi. It doesn't matter what we choose for our morning reading; only that we choose and read something.

After reading, we can take a few extra moments to reflect upon how the subject matter pertains to our everyday life. Is there a connection between what we read and how we currently feel, or what is going on in our life? Did something in the reading resonate with us? To spend a few moments pondering over this gives our spiritual/intuitive muscles some much-needed exercise. And a word to those among us with addictive tendencies: Rather than choose four or five readings each morning, it is better to pick one or two and then take time to digest the messages they impart.

Take pen in hand

To take another couple of minutes to jot down a few thoughts about what we have read further increases our chances for replacing old distorted and perhaps doubting messages with new, more positive thoughts. We can buy ourselves a journal specifically for this purpose. Often, once we start writing, more is revealed as we are provided clarity not our own.

The way in which we
begin our day will
determine how well
(or not) we will live it.

If we have difficulty knowing how to begin this journaling exercise, we might start with a simple, "Good morning, God," or "Good morning, Spirit," or "Good morning, Higher Self." We could follow this up by summarizing what we have read, or writing about our concerns regarding the upcoming day. Or we could use this time to really start the day on a positive note by compiling a gratitude list, thanking the Universe for the many gifts in our lives.

Come "apart-from"

Another great way to slow down and connect with the "Real" is by taking ourselves apart from our normal routines every now and then. We can attend a spiritual retreat or a Body/Soul conference. Whether they last a day, a weekend, or a week, both offer affordable and gentle ways for us to shift our focus, quiet our mind, share with other like-minded persons, and, most often, to feel the presence of Divine Life-Giving Energy.

Spending time at a spa can also be a spiritual practice, especially when we make mindfulness our intention. Being on the receiving end of a massage, facial, or body wrap helps us to momentarily slow both mental and physical busyness so that we can connect with our heart space, to our soul, to where our spirit resides.

Other ways to open our heart and connect with the *Real* include spending time in nature, camping, hiking, beach-walking, drumming, chanting, dancing, drawing, creating most anything, attending various religious services, even visiting a planetarium. All are capable of moving us into a deeper state of authentic being.

None of these suggestions requires anything more than a willingness to take them. So look them over again. Then consider which one(s) you are prepared to take on at this point in your life. Remember, we are working on balance and boundaries and this chapter is guaranteed to help us in both of those regards—and infinitely more...

Exercise 16: Open and Discover

Come up with at least one new practice for your spiritual life (which in turn will bring you into greater balance). For instance, I am willing to:

- Develop a morning routine.
- Invite the Higher Power/Higher Good into my life.
- Watch less television.
- Read more that is inspirational.
- Create a special "quiet place."
- Give journaling a try.
- Listen to music that resonates with my soul.
- Spend time in nature.
- Go on a spiritual retreat.
- Join a drumming class.
- Attend a body/soul conference.

- Incorporate chanting into my life.
- Get a massage, facial, or reflexology.
- Begin or continue with yoga.

Don't just write down what you are planning to do; make arrangements to do it! Sign up for that class. Look for the music. Buy a new journal. Create your sacred space. Register for the conference. Find a retreat. Take one intentional step in this new direction and do it now while you are thinking about it.

Once we begin walking in a new direction, the benefits will be felt almost immediately. Provided we keep an open mind and take active steps to recover our spiritual center, we will be amazed at the results. We will begin to change in ways both small and large. Feelings of well-being and clarity will increase. We will become more attuned to the enormous wealth of wisdom and insight contained within us. Our belief in something greater/eternal/unchanging will take on new proportions and meaning. We will feel far more balanced and serene. *We will begin to realize that spiritual energy and intuition are our greatest resources.*

Reading and writing in the morning helps remove old messages and replace them with new and more positive thoughts.

Chapter Fifteen: Expand Awareness

Although some spiritual awakenings are sudden and profound, most occur gradually over time. In fact, the process can take place without our even being aware of it. One day we just realize that there is much more *to* us and *beyond* us. Instead of feeling quite so alone, frantic, or fearful, we feel calm, centered, and wide awake. However, we cannot rest on our laurels. The spiritual life is not for those who want it or even for those who need it. *It is for those who are willing to put in the time and effort necessary to recover our divine inner spark and to connect with the Real.*

This involves ever-expanding our awareness and understanding. None of this is a quick fix, so without a doubt, it will be the men and women who long the deepest and who suffer the greatest cosmic unrest who will be most likely to incorporate these new behaviors. If you are among those, you are the lucky ones; for you will increase your chances tenfold for recovering and discovering those rooms within yourself which have long been waiting for this moment in time.

Following are some additional measures we can take to assist us in this journey.

Find a spiritual friend/mentor

Our own spiritual journey is often enhanced by like-minded friends and helpmates. In fact, our own process of "coming to believe" may have begun by believing that they believed! So we look for those who have what we want—serenity, clarity, and the joy of living. We look for friends who "walk the talk" and who appear to be comfortable in their own skins regardless of circumstances; those whose lives embody an honesty and generosity of spirit which can only come from an authentic spiritual connection. We call upon these people for hope, support, or guidance when we are full of doubt. We allow their belief to carry us when we don't have our own.

Working with a spiritual director can also be helpful for deepening one's spiritual journey. However, spiritual guidance is not always easy to find. We must be careful as we don't want to wind up with a charlatan, or with somebody whose primary purpose is to convert us to their beliefs. Probably the safest way to find a qualified spiritual director is to contact local retreat houses for a list. We don't need to commit to the first person we speak with, but can meet with several until we find one with whom we feel safe, understood, and with whom we "connect."

Ask for what you need

We initially began our spiritual recovery with a prayer of invitation. And although this was a great beginning, if we wish to journey into a deeper, more authentic spirituality, we must take our prayer life one step further. As Mohandas K. Gandhi so aptly put it, "Prayer is not an old woman's idle amusement. Properly understood, it is the most potent instrument of action." In other words, it not only helps to unlock and open those many rooms within us, but it also moves mountains.

Still, despite all of these promises, some of us may continue to be resistant. Maybe we think we have already tried prayer to no avail. Or perhaps the circumstances of our lives seem so unjust that prayer feels out of the question. Maybe we are in such pain that we couldn't pray even if we wanted to. Or perhaps we have been taught that it is selfish to pray for our own ends.

Or maybe, if we really looked closely, we would find that our biggest problem with prayer has been thinking that we know what is best. Perhaps we are so accustomed to imploring God time after time to give us specific outcomes, that when these prayers aren't answered in the way we desire, we make the assumption that prayer doesn't work. In reality, if we cast a discerning eye back over our lives, would we not find that in so many cases, the wisdom of the Universe generated much better long-term results than our short-sighted desires might have?

Did we ever stop to consider that maybe we've been in the habit of asking for the wrong things? That instead of imploring some Higher Power for specific answers and outcomes—to win the lottery, have the guy or gal fall madly in love with us, or to get the job—we could ask for things like *courage* to open our heart, *patience* with our co-workers, *willingness* to go on the interview, *guidance* to make the best decision, *restraint* from acting on our impulses, *perseverance* to keep on keeping on? We might even write the question in our journal, "What do I need from God/Higher Power/Universal Energy today?", and be honest with our answers.

After we ask for exactly what we need, we can go one step further by acting "as if" our prayers were going to be answered. This requires action which is not based upon *feelings*, but upon making a decision. In other words, we can be full of fear or huge insecurity or have no faith whatsoever, but still make the decision to take action in accordance with what we have asked for. This is about suiting up and showing up, taking a leap of faith in the face of our anxieties. It is not easy! But if we can take the risk to do it anyway, to step off the cliff, chances are good that a ledge will appear or we will be given the wings to fly. And as difficult as doing this might be, it is the only way that we will ever find out that prayer really works.

Create a mantra

A most helpful tool for acting "as if," especially in the face of high stress or anxiety, is the use of a personal mantra. A mantra is a word or phrase that is repeated over and over again, requiring our full attention. Often used as a basis for deep meditation, mantras also come in handy for stopping anxiety before it has the opportunity to build up full steam.

Mantras can be anything we want them to be. Sometimes their phrases resonate with our personal belief system and sometimes they are simply expressions that bring us peace. For example:

- My heart is filled with love.
- I trust and rely on God.
- I release all fear and doubt.
- I am not alone.

If we take the risk to
step off the cliff, it can be
guaranteed that a ledge
will appear or we will be
given the wings to fly.

- Easy does it.
- All is well.

Repeating any of these phrases over and over in our mind, or even aloud, can become a spiritual practice, one that reduces our anxiety and brings us more into the now.

Exercise 17: Choose and Use

If you were to choose or come up with your own personal mantra, what would it be? Take a moment to give some thought as to what might work well for you. Write it down. Use this mantra whenever you begin to feel any kind of stress, anxiety, or doubt; or when you want to bring yourself back into the now. Repeating the phrase over and over again will restore calmness and clarity.

Our prayer life can be a practice that grows and evolves in wonderful ways. We begin by inviting the Higher Energy into our daily lives and concerns. We ask for what we need, for ourselves and for others; perhaps in the beginning by uttering one simple word in earnest: "Please." We then act "as if" by taking whatever action is necessary to assist the Higher Power/Higher Consciousness in realizing these goals and wishes. The more spiritually attuned we become, the more likely these goals will be aligned with what's best for all concerned. This is especially true when we remain mindful of the greatest prayer of all, that of "Thank you." Nothing moves us towards "what really matters"

Prayer not only helps to
unlock and open those many
rooms within us, but it
also moves mountains.

more than this. So we practice gratitude in all of our affairs, and draw closer to what is real.

Once we develop some practice and continuity around our prayer life, we will want to find ways to pay attention as our requests will most assuredly be answered in one form or another. However, because they may not be answered in the ways we expect, we must stay vigilant as to not miss the miracles! The following exercise will help us.

Exercise 18: Pay Attention

Provided we start the day with prayer of some kind, a good way to pay attention to how these prayers are answered is by doing a short review of our day before going to bed. We might ask ourselves questions such as:

- Did my day go more smoothly because I started it off with prayer/reflection?
- Was I given clarity regarding a situation that had me confused?
- Did I have a prayer answered, even though it may not have been answered in the way in which I had hoped?
- Did I worry less today because I asked a Higher Power for help with a specific problem?
- Was I able to take a risk, to stretch myself to do or say something that would normally intimidate or frighten me?
- Did I experience more serenity than usual?

- Did I find things for which to be grateful throughout the day? Would it be beneficial to work on this more?
- Where else might I have noticed the presence of something Greater than Myself?

The more committed we become to our morning routine and the more habitual with this nightly inventory, the greater our chances of experiencing the Divine in ways we can't even imagine at this point.

Chapter Sixteen: Move Beyond the Chatter

Next to prayer, the most beneficial spiritual practice we can develop is that of finding ways to move beyond the chatter. Some of us may be so accustomed to noisiness and incessant distraction that even the thought of becoming still can make us squirm. Our immediate reaction might be to think that it's too difficult, we don't have the time to get quiet, we don't know how, or what's the point anyway? Once again, this is our fear and doubt trying to sabotage our attempts at connecting with the Real. And as we know by now, sometimes the only way to get beyond these saboteurs is by kicking our resistance and excuses to the curb and taking the next right action in spite of them.

In this case, the next right action involves cultivating silence; taking the time to cease all outer activity and attempt to quiet our mind and emotions, which in some cases have not been calm for eons. But today is a new day, and becoming still is essential for expanding our spiritual awareness and gaining access to our heart/soul space which has so long eluded us; that inner world full of information, wisdom, and intuition. At the same time, silence opens the channels for us to hear the small, still voice of our Higher Power, Higher Consciousness. After all, it would be a rather one-sided relationship if we did all the talking!

So we practice sitting quietly, just as if we were waiting for a butterfly to come light upon our shoulder. We focus on our breath going in and out, or on a single word such as "Om." This is meditation and it is vital in our quest to live consciously and serenely. Meditation is able to move us beyond and beneath the chatter of the world and, especially, of our ever-active minds. Temporarily removing us from secular distractions, meditation provides freedom and relief from our "cosmic unrest." It empowers us to see beyond the obvious. Meditation expands our consciousness and keeps us right-sized. It is the primary vehicle by which we "get over ourselves to find our Selves."

Think about a raging sea with a choppy surface complete with huge waves and high winds. It can be chaotic, frightening and distracting, to say the least. Meditation allows us to move far beneath this tumultuous surface to a deep inner calm; a place where everything becomes clear and calm. And there are many different ways of achieving this movement. Some techniques focus explicitly on the breath, others use the repetition of a single word, phrase, or sound such as "Om," and still others consist of guided imagery. There are books, tapes, and videos that explain and demonstrate ways in which we can become centered and still. In the beginning, it might prove beneficial to use one of these, or to join an ongoing meditation group. Practices such as tai chi, yoga, and qigong all place an emphasis on quieting oneself by going within.

The only thing we really need in order to meditate is the willingness to give it a try—and then the added willingness to persevere with our attempts. This may not be easy, especially in the beginning. Chances are, that the moment we try to quiet our racing thoughts, all kinds of inner and outer distractions will begin competing for our attention. Instead of becoming quieter and calmer, we may initially feel the exact opposite— our bodies may fidget, we may feel restless, or we may even experience a momentary increase in anxiety. At the same time, our minds can begin to

Meditation helps us
"get over ourselves"
in order to find ourselves.

gravitate towards the negative—old pain, fear, and unresolved issues can begin rising to the surface of our consciousness. Getting beyond these will be especially challenging during our early forays into meditation. However, this is a process which always gets easier and more beneficial with time and practice. Always.

Finding a meditation practice that suits us is often a whole lot easier than finding the time and space to accommodate it. Let's face it; few of us have much extra time within our days to do something like meditate. If this is the case, we must do what we can to create some. We might revisit our T.E.A. chart in the beginning of this book and take something else off the "outgoing energy" side in order to put prayer and meditation on the "incoming" side. Meditation doesn't require a huge block of time. A good goal to aim for is twenty minutes a day in which to begin. If we can't find twenty, we can start with ten. If we can't find ten minutes, five minutes is better than nothing. We can set a timer and just do it!

Not only do we need to figure out *when* we can meditate, but it is also helpful to have an idea of *where* to do it. Just as with our prayer life, we want a space in which we will be undisturbed, warm, and comfortable. Once again, we want to set ourselves up for success!

Becoming still and quieting our mind and emotions is some of the most important work we will ever do. For cultivating silence is the only way we can truly hear that small voice within us, as well as the voice of that which is Eternal. We learn to listen and we listen to learn. It is in this silence, in the stillness, in the listening, that we find what we truly seek.

If we're not willing
to go within,
we're bound to go without.

If we want to see clearly, we must close our eyes and move within. And if we're not willing to go within, then we are definitely bound to *go without.*

As we persist in our efforts to connect with our inner world, to cultivate spiritual wisdom, intuition, and energy, we must bear in mind that while some positive benefits will be realized almost immediately, our journey into the *Real* will unfold and unfurl in stages. Bit by bit, new layers, new insight, and new understanding will be revealed. Slowly but surely, our innate intuition will become sharpened, our senses heightened, our wisdom revived. It will be as if we have put on a new set of eye glasses, not distorted or murky, but ones that allow us to look beyond all that doesn't make sense and see the many things that do. At the same time, we will become more balanced, feel more confident, and enjoy greater serenity and joy. Our energy will increase in leaps and bounds. Our ability to deal with life's ups and downs will astonish even us.

As we continue to uncover, recover, and connect, our belief in "Something" greater than ourselves will take on new meaning. We will begin to notice how the right people and the right circumstances seem to be placed in our path almost as if by design. Individual and invisible hands will show up at the most opportune times, and we will begin to recognize these "coincidences" as being the Universe's way of showing support.

And even in those moments when we briefly fall back into feeling uniquely separate and alone, down deep we will know differently. For we will have recovered what we have so long been looking for; the intuitive conviction that we are indeed connected—to everything that ever was, everything that presently is, and to everything yet to come. It's eternal. It's Real. It's all good. And it's all possible.

<u>Reader Commitment to Connecting with the Real</u>

In order to work on a spiritual journey, I commit to the following:

_____

_____

_____

Today's date:_____

Notes on Part Four

_____

_____

_____

_____

_____

_____

_____

_____

_____

_____

_____

_____

_____

_____

_____

_____

_____

_____

_____

_____

_____

_____

_____

_____

_____

_____

_____

_____

Epilogue: Now What?

You have reached the end of this first book in the trilogy of *Busy Person's Guides.* If you have done the exercises and taken the suggestions as presented, you are undoubtedly enjoying some good positive results of your actions.

Ideally, you have freed up some time in your busy lifestyle, becoming more realistic about what can and cannot be accomplished in a day. You have made your to-do list manageable by learning how to delegate and/ or question, "How important is it?" At the same time, you have taken steps to increase your self-care; not by whipping yourself into shape, but by nurturing yourself into well-being. You have realized the benefits of slowing down, taking time to reflect and consider, spending quality "me-time," and asking yourself, "What really matters?" Finally— you can *breathe.*

When it comes to letting go, you now have clear-cut directions for releasing emotional baggage. You understand the underlying process for letting go, and have used it to take your power and energy back. Resentment, regret, worry, disappointment and the like, no longer call the shots on how you feel in any given day or moment. Instead of struggling to get rid of these negative emotions, you can experience the freedom and ease which come as a result of simply walking in the opposite direction. Your emotional heaviness has been exchanged for the lightness of being. Bravo!

You have also taken measures to establish some good healthy boundaries. Using your new boundary "toolkit," you no longer say "yes" when everything in you screams "no," thus avoiding the pitfalls of feeling resentful and/or taken advantage of. You have learned how to put the ball back in *their* court when need be, realizing that it is not your job to fix, micromanage, or do for others what they clearly need to be doing for themselves. You have tools for saying what you mean and meaning what you say without saying it meanly. You have recovered valuable energy, and your relationships have improved as a result, including your relationship with yourself.

Where your spiritual life is concerned, you have hopefully kicked your resistance to the curb and stepped over and beyond your many misconceptions and preconceptions. By making a decision to be open-minded and willing to do what needs to be done, you have been given carte blanche for discovering your own path for connecting with the *Real.* If you have followed suggestions and taken time to enter into the silence, chances are good that you have come face to face with at least a glimpse of your own true Self. At the same time, you have undoubtedly heard the whisper of the Universe responding to your many questions. How wonderful to have embarked upon the journey of discovering who you really are and what really is your purpose!

So now what? You have finished reading this book and that is a great accomplishment for sure, especially if you have done the exercises as well. In fact, at this point, you might want to take a minute to go back and review your four Reader Commitments. Are you staying true to your own intentions for change? If so, that is terrific. If not, there is no reason to beat yourself up over it. It may be that you need to make a readjustment in your lifestyle in order to better accommodate these goals. This is to be expected. So don't be in a hurry to move on. Take your time. In fact, you might even want to go through this book again, this time doing the exercises with a close friend or in a group. If you do, be prepared to discover new information about yourself, as more will definitely be revealed each time you make the journey through these pages.

As stated in the beginning, this book on balance and boundaries is also your preparation for *The Busy Person's Guide to Inner Healing*. In this sequel, you will come face to face with another kind of work; that of identifying, facing, and moving through those underlying issues which may be driving and draining you in the first place! It would only stand to reason that the more in balance you can be, the greater your ability to address this very necessary work of inner healing.

So take a breath. Sit back. Relax but hold onto your seat. You have done a good job thus far in preparing yourself to continue this marvelous process of discovery, of seeking and accessing those many rooms inside of you; a process with the ultimate goal of finding your own true voice and your authentic place in the greater scheme of things—transported and transformed into a reality where you will feel whole, useful, satisfied, and content, able to appreciate on a daily basis the joy that really is in the journey.

Welcome.

About the Author

Referred to as "the real deal," Betty Hill Crowson is the author of *The Joy is in the Journey: A Woman's Guide through Crisis and Change* (Authorhouse, 2005), as well as a motivational speaker, retreat director, holistic life coach, and human growth-potential specialist. For the past two decades, she has become known and appreciated, especially throughout the Northeast, for her charismatic speaking style and her unusual ability to combine traditional and current wisdom-knowledge into easily understood and practical concepts. Her workshops, spiritual retreats, and tele-classes under the trademark of The Joy is in the Journey® are highly in demand and reviewed as "life-changing" by participants. Betty currently spends her time between Shelter Island, NY, and the mountains of Western Maine. More information about Betty and the work she offers can be obtained at www.thejoyisinthejourney.com